Who Is Blues Volume 1

Doug MacLeod

The authorized compact biography

VINCENT ABBATE

Who Is Blues Volume 1: Doug MacLeod

All photos courtesy of Doug MacLeod except where noted.
Front cover photo © Theo Looijmans
Back cover photo © Jeff Fasano
Book design by Joseph Abbate
Lyrics reprinted with the kind permission of Gaslight Square Music.
Lyrics from “Break The Chain” reprinted with the kind permission of Gaslight Square Music and I Swear I'm Not From The South.

ISBN-10: 1721731679
ISBN-13: 978-1721731671

For information contact:
Who Is Blues
www.whoisblues.com

For all the road dogs.

CONTENTS

BLUE NOTES

Dresden, Germany. A Sunday morning in the spring of 2002. A music-filled weekend is winding down in a room full of exhausted souls. Festival organizers, media people, musicians and a few odd stragglers, all of whom have pretty much had their fill of the goddamn blues.

Except there's this man seated onstage, a National Reso-Phonic guitar propped on his knee. The one he calls Mule. He's the reason they've dragged their dog-tired bodies out of bed. The visiting musician has already played two shows on the weekend, but no one who heard his stories and songs the first or the second time around wants to miss this semi-private command performance.

An onlooker is watching him from the back of the room, his whole world in a state of flux. He has never heard blues this powerful, music so full of pain and longing and hope and humanity that it shakes him to the core.

Across the room, more toward the front, there is a woman. She, too, is feeling it.

Something is pulling these two souls together. Calling them to one another.

The man at the back can't believe he is falling in love. He won't allow it. He is committed to another. That love – the old love – has withered. He knows that. And yet, to let it go, to risk opening himself to this unexpected new love, fills him with fear and sorrow and apprehension. He does not know what to do.

As if somehow tuned into the onlooker's inner turmoil, the man onstage presses the brass slide he wears on the pinky finger of his left hand against the six strings of his guitar, coaxes a mournful cry from its wooden body and begins to sing.

I believe to my soul it's time for a change...

Doug MacLeod is the subject of Who Is Blues Volume 1 and that is no accident. But it's not because he's a multiple Blues Music Award winner or for any of the other achievements of his roughly 50 years as a musician. That weekend in Dresden – my first encounter with MacLeod's music – literally altered the course of my life. The onlooker was me. The guitarist was Doug. The song was "Time For A Change."

At the time, I had no idea of the emotional

hardship he had to endure as a child. Perhaps it's what made him gravitate to this music we call the blues. Nor had I heard the stories of the older generation blues men and women who showed him, with tough love, how to harness whatever he was feeling inside so that listeners could feel it, too.

All I knew was that his music spoke to me. In fact, on that life-changing morning in Dresden, it caused me to flee the room in a hurry. I didn't want the others to see me crying.

I've met, interviewed, shared a beer and talked baseball with Doug many times since then – most recently during a festival in Hamburg, Germany, where we conducted most of the interviews for the book you are now holding. There, I watched others – newcomers to Doug MacLeod – have reactions similar to the one I had sixteen years ago, like the gangly, bespectacled keyboard player who passed me on the stairs after Doug's set, shaking his head in amazement at what he'd just witnessed.

With this book, I hope to bring you a little bit closer to the man. I've tried to stay out of the way as much as possible and let Doug tell his story. I hope you feel his spirit.

Vincent Abbate
July 2018

GUEST SPOT:
JORMA KAUKONEN

When I first met Doug MacLeod and heard him play at our Fur Peace Ranch, I was more than stunned. I couldn't believe I had not tuned in to him much earlier. I realized I was in the presence of one of the great blues artists . . . period!

His passion and purity moved me almost beyond words. His playing is powerful, emotional and yet precise. The stories he tells with his voice wrap you in his world until the last note.

In an era filled with commercial glitz, his stories need to be heard. His groove is so deep you almost need a shovel to get out. I'm obviously a big fan and you need to make a listening appointment with his work right now. Doug is most definitely one of our most significant blues artists . . . and he is a noble human being. I'm tuned in now!

Jorma Kaukonen
Rock and Roll Hall of Fame inductee / Jefferson Airplane
February 2018

"That darkness that I've had my whole life,
I've channeled it through the music into something
positive. Even in the biggest pile of manure,
a rose can grow. Music is my rose."

ORIGINS

Ghosts walking in a mist of lies.

The phrase – coined by Doug MacLeod for a song called "Break The Chain" – expresses one man's fractured relationship to his own, distant past. To shadowy figures with twisted imaginations. To unseemly events that blotted out the joy of the little boy. His dim memories of life in the 1940s and 1950s are shrouded in mystery and deception.

"Honestly, I can't tell you like most people can tell," he shrugs, trying to recall details of his childhood and family history.

To begin with, MacLeod – now in his seventies, his head crowned with wispy white hair – is unsure of his own ethnicity. For most of his life, he believed his heritage to be 100% Scottish. It's what his parents told him and it's what he told anyone who asked. Later, he came to realize there is Acadian DNA inside him as well, passed on via ancestors from the Maritime Provinces of Canada.

Moreover, the blues veterans he ran with in 1970s Los Angeles were certain he had “black blood” coursing through his veins – not just because of the kinky mullet he wore back then or his darker than pale complexion. “I really can’t say for sure. What I can say is I always felt comfortable on the other side of the tracks.”

In particular, he recalls a conversation with his friend and mentor George “Harmonica” Smith.

“Once, George came up to me and said, ‘Dubb’ – that’s what he always called me – ‘Dubb, I don’t mean no insult, but I gotta ask you something. You know, you don’t play guitar like a white man. And you don’t sing like a white man. And sometimes you don’t even act like a white man. Are you sure you’re a white man?’”

Actually, he isn’t.

“What difference would it make? Would it make a difference if I had, say, sixteen percent black blood in me as opposed to ten percent? Would that make a difference in how I play?” By now, MacLeod has accepted his inability to know what came before him as a condition of his upbringing.

“There were so many lies in my family.”

He laughs often in conversation, so amused in the telling of his favorite tales that he frequently breaks off his sentences to let all the laughing out.

This is not one of those moments. MacLeod's voice is steady and sober.

"So many lies that we will never find out the truth."

But he does wonder about the things he doesn't understand. Like why he was born in New York. The family home at the time of his birth in April of 1946 was in the Raleigh-Durham area of North Carolina. MacLeod's earliest boyhood memories are of fishing off the end of a pier with a bamboo pole and a red and white bobber.

"But just before I was born, like three weeks before, my father took us all up to New York to stay with my aunt. I was born in Manhattan. Then, when I was a month old, we moved back to Raleigh. A year and a half later my brother was born. My father took us all up to New York to stay with my aunt. My mother gave birth to my brother in New York and we all moved back to North Carolina. The only reason I know that much is because my mother told me."

MacLeod's mother, Dorothy "Dutchie" MacLeod (née Cameron), never explained why.

"My wife Patti heard this story and couldn't believe it. Once, we were sitting with my mother – she was getting old, getting set to leave – and I truly believe that when people get to that point, they wanna travel light, so there's not a lot in the suitcase. My wife asked her:

'Dutchie, is it true that Doug was conceived in North Carolina?'

She said yes.

'And you took the family up to New York to have him born there and then went back down to Raleigh?'

My mother said yes.

'And you did the same thing when Bruce was born?'"

Dorothy MacLeod confirmed the superficial details of this unique family ritual, but closed the window on the past when pressed for reasons. Instead of opening up to her daughter-in-law, Dutchie MacLeod politely offered her a cup of tea.

"It was as close to the truth as she wanted to give out," MacLeod reasons.

Still, vague memories remain of fishing as a small boy and of the household he shared with his mother, his younger brother Bruce and his father William "Bally" MacLeod, a proud Canadian immigrant who made a very good living as a successful businessman, one who expected his two boys to continue his climb up the social ladder.

Music first entered his eldest son's consciousness in the form of Louis Jordan, the pioneering rhythm and blues bandleader who helped pave the way for rock and roll with a series of swinging singles in the 1940s and 1950s. Again, MacLeod relays memories passed along to him by his mom.

"When we lived in North Carolina," he explains, "there was a neighbor that loved Louis Jordan's music. He would come home after work – he was a manual laborer – take a shower, have his supper, then go to his music room, which was real close to where my bedroom was as a little boy. He would turn up his Louis Jordan records and have a wonderful time. My mother was worried if her little boy was getting any sleep. She told me she went into the bedroom to check on me. And there I was, with my eyes closed and my little foot moving."

When MacLeod was about seven, the family relocated north. This time it was for more than a few weeks. They settled for a while in Port Washington, New York, an affluent community on the north shore of Long Island. Then – as now – the town ranked among the wealthiest places in America (and reportedly served as F. Scott Fitzgerald's model for East Egg in *The Great Gatsby*), but MacLeod doesn't recall his family ever hobnobbing with the super-rich.

"We were upper middle-class, I'd say. We certainly weren't poor. We didn't need for anything. But we weren't Guggenheims."

Once again, fishing is part of the childhood tableau. "We trawled for striped bass on a little dinghy with a five horsepower motor on it." He also remembers being drawn to the home of a famous singer who lived in nearby Sands Point.

"Perry Como lived there. When we were kids, that's where we wanted to go for Halloween, because there was always lots of candy at Perry Como's house."

As innocent as all this sounds, there were secrets lurking beneath the surface – traumatic occurrences he would only learn about later in life – that turned young Doug into a stutterer. Small traces of it remain in his speech even today, barely noticeable, but back then, the stammer was so extreme he chose never to open his mouth. He hid in his room most of the time, away from people, afraid to answer the phone. He felt like he would never fit in, never find a friend, never be able to ask a girl out on a date.

The rock and roll of the late 1950s was all about teenagers in love. The Everly Brothers, The Coasters and Bobby Darin dominated the AM radio airwaves as MacLeod grew into adolescence. He gravitated to the music and – at around the age of 13 – picked up the bass guitar to improve his chances with the opposite sex. If they wouldn't give him the time of day at school or around town, he figured maybe they'd notice him on the bandstand. Once he had the basics down, Doug joined a band called The Fliptones. The early returns were promising, so he stuck with it.

Then it was time to move again. This time to the Midwest. The MacLeods left Long Island and put down stakes in Warson Woods, a quiet residential area in St. Louis County, Missouri, some 15 miles west of downtown St. Louis. It was there, on the western bank of the Mississippi River, that MacLeod first experienced the power of the blues.

"A buddy of mine named Steve Waldman asked me if I wanted to go hear some blues. I said no, let's go hear some doo-wop, let's go hear some rock and roll." But his friend didn't let up. He knew of some live music clubs in the black part of town, told Doug he didn't know what he was missing.

"So we went down there together and saw one of those great St. Louis bands that most people don't know about. It must have been someone like Eugene Neal or Benny Sharp. I went, 'Wow!'"

MacLeod, still a fledgling bassist, soon hooked up with an outfit named Eddie Lewis & The Starfires. The band would play teen dances and sock hops, often backing up local rhythm and blues and rock and roll singers.

"We were clean, you know," he laughs. "We had the skinny suits with the skinny ties, the Beatle-type boots and everything. And we had those synchronized moves. Back then, if you played, you had to move."

He vividly recalls The Starfires backing up St. Louis native and rock and roll trailblazer Chuck Berry at a recreation hall affiliated with Mosley Electronics – a landmark occasion for more than the obvious reasons.

"We were done with our set when this girl came up to me. This was back in the days of teased hair. She was a real knockout. She asked me if I was in the band. I said yeah. 'What do you do in the band?' I told her I was the bass player. She says 'oh' and moves on to the guitar player, who at that time was the third ugliest guy on the planet. And there were five women around him! Buzzin' on him! I turned to Gene Gray, the saxophone player, and told him I was giving up bass. I thought, if that guy can get five women, I can at least get one."

MacLeod's guitar skills were limited at that point, so he made the hormone-driven decision to work hard on improving his chops. He grabbed whatever guitar gigs he could find, the blues slowly but surely becoming a more comfortable environment for him.

"But I still had that stutter. I still really couldn't speak."

For some reason, he decided one day to try singing. "And *this* voice came out. A different voice than the one I had. I said to myself, I'm taking the voice that doesn't stutter. Wherever it came from, I could sing the blues. With authority. I could always sing it with this voice."

More than a half-century later, MacLeod looks back at his blues initiation in St. Louis with gratitude and wonder. Why should this awkward white kid from the suburbs, one who felt out of place everywhere else, feel so at home among people who were not his own?

"I was welcome from the first moment I walked into those clubs. I wasn't scared. I shoulda been. Those were rough places."

The music itself spoke to him in a strangely familiar language.

"I heard it and gravitated to it. I felt like that's where I was supposed to be."

At home, no one understood. William MacLeod in particular did not appreciate what he viewed as his son's slumming.

"I think it was tough for my father to accept it. He was above the middle class. He had moved up. And here is his son, playing what he called 'Negro music' and being attracted to a social group that was many steps down economically."

In the blues, MacLeod had stumbled upon something that gave him purpose and a sense of belonging. But it wasn't enough. The stifling environment at home became too much for him. "I just couldn't live there anymore. I just couldn't be there."

Several months before his 18th birthday, he found a way out by pre-enlisting in the U.S. Navy. His actual hitch began in the summer of 1964. He calls it his legal way of running away from home.

"I was so desperate to leave that I went down to the courthouse in Clayton, Missouri. There were two lines. One was for the Marines. One was for the Navy. I picked the shortest line."

Given that United States troop deployment in Vietnam mushroomed from roughly 23,000 in 1963 to almost 185,000 a year later and would double again by the end of 1966, MacLeod's spur of the moment decision was borderline reckless. Though in retrospect, he certainly chose the right line at the courthouse.

"God almighty, if I had picked the Marines, I probably wouldn't be sitting here today."

As it is, he never once left the continental US during his four-year tour of duty. Following boot camp in San Diego, MacLeod was sent to the Naval Air Station in Millington, Tennessee, just north of Memphis, and eventually wound up in Norfolk, Virginia, home to the largest naval base in the world. His extraordinary skill in repairing the APS 88, a common type of radar unit, kept him in port for the remainder of his military service.

"I was a savant, believe it or not," he laughs. "I was getting radars sent to me from all up and down the East Coast. From Bangor, Maine to Jacksonville, Florida, whatever the other guys couldn't fix, they sent to me. That's what kept me off the Forrestal when it left the Atlantic Fleet to join the Pacific Fleet in Vietnam, where they had that accident." The fire and series of explosions aboard the USS Forrestal in July of 1967 killed 134 of his fellow sailors, injuring dozens more. "It kept the First Class Petty Officer in charge of the shop off the ship as well; they wanted us to be together so we could fix these radars."

Norfolk looms large in MacLeod's history for other reasons. His job at the radar repair shop was, for the most part, a nine-to-five job. Nights and weekends, he was busy making the rounds of the city's lively folk music scene. Think hippies, coffeehouses, widespread drug use. Doug lived off base and fancied himself a player.

"There was a big folk scene there. Emmylou Harris was playing back then. Juice Newton. John Carlini, the excellent jazz musician from New York, was playing. Jim Dawson, the folk singer. I was a blues guy."

And, he admits today, rather full of himself. He thought showing up at the clubs in threadbare jeans, beat-up shoes and a guitar case he had scraped on a brick wall to make it look like he'd been hoboing would magically turn him into a bluesman.

Then someone offered to introduce him to a guitarist who had barrelhoused with Blind Lemon Jefferson, the seminal Texas songster who was one of the blues' first recorded superstars. By now, MacLeod was sure of his blues cred. So he agreed to visit the man at his home.

"I was gonna go up there and show him how great I was."

That man was Ernest Banks.

* * *

Anyone who has ever attended a Doug MacLeod performance will have heard of him. Generally,

MacLeod invokes the name of Ernest Banks in connection with the twofold musical philosophy "the old man" drilled into him:

1) Never play a note you don't believe, and

2) Never write or sing about what you don't know about.

Banks was MacLeod's first teacher and immeasurably impacted the music he would make further down the road, yet Doug knows even less of his origins than of his own.

"I don't think Ernest Banks was his real name," he says of the man he describes as small and wide, with chocolate skin, a head like a bowling ball and one eye. "I think he was somebody else and probably did something in Mississippi or Texas – maybe he shot somebody – and migrated up to Virginia. He didn't play in the Piedmont style like Blind Blake and those guys. He played like a tough Texas or Mississippi guy. So I'm not really sure who he was. But I'm sure he could play."

Banks lived in isolation in a wooded area near the village of Toano, Virginia. To get there, MacLeod would cross the James River from Norfolk, head a good fifty miles up Highway 60 in his rust-colored Volkswagen Beetle, drive another five miles or so from the interstate, then off toward the Little Creek

Reservoir. Banks lived near what is now called Chickahominy Road.

"Back then, you had to know which magnolia tree to turn right at to go back in the woods to find him."

The old man, a widower, had fallen on hard times.

"He had a two-story house, but it was all tore down except for the kitchen. That's where he lived. His bed was in the kitchen. There was a linoleum and metal kind of table. And a little dog named Lemon."

The first thing he learned from Banks was a bit of bluesman etiquette: "If you're visiting someone's house, you bring them something." As long as he didn't show up empty-handed, like he did on his first trip out to Toano, MacLeod was welcome to come around whenever he wanted.

"I think what Ernest saw was a young man with a lot of feeling and a lot of soul who was a jive-ass guitar player. So he wanted to teach me to play what really counts."

Like so many musicians raised in the pious environment of the South, Banks preferred to sing spirituals and needed a beer or two in him before he would consent to play the blues. Then he would show his aspiring pupil a few songs and answer questions about the particular guitar tunings he used. He explained the importance of what MacLeod calls the dead thumb right-hand rhythm. Banks schooled him in the fundamentals of entertainment and what it takes to get a crowd going.

"He told me you gotta sound like you're more than one guy up there, that you gotta have it all going on. If you got a guy up there and his playing is what I call 'museum' playing, no woman is going to dance to that. And if the women aren't dancing, the men ain't buying them drinks. And if the men ain't spending money, then you ain't gettin' paid."

Banks' technical explanations were fairly rudimentary. MacLeod often couldn't understand his unique backwoods dialect. And yet, it was during those regular visits that the young poser from the Norfolk coffeehouses slowly began to grasp what the blues could be.

"What he taught me was the honesty of this music. That it's about being who you are and what you are. The stuff about never play or sing about what you don't know about. Powerful shit."

He often wondered why Banks chose him as a vessel for his knowledge. Doug believes there was more to it than simply showing up at his house regularly with a six-pack of Pabst Blue Ribbon.

"I do wonder why he gave me the chance. Maybe it was because of my childhood. I could relate to the suffering and pain. The blues spoke to me. Even back then, I could always sing this music."

* * *

While immersing himself in the blues through Ernest Banks, MacLeod was also busy discovering jazz. In particular, he had fallen hard for Kenny Burrell, the prolific, Detroit-born electric guitarist who had recorded more than two dozen albums by the mid-1960s. To this day, Burrell is among his favorite musicians.

"I heard Kenny Burrell and thought, I would love to do that." So when MacLeod's four-year hitch with the Navy ended in 1968, rather than carry on as an acoustic blues performer, he decided to see if there was a jazz player inside of him. One seemingly impossible hurdle: He couldn't read musical notation.

Still, in 1969, following a semester at the University of Missouri-St. Louis, he managed to get accepted to the illustrious Berklee School of Music in Boston, thanks to a recommendation from Don James, a Hammond B3 player who was a friend of St. Louis composer Oliver Nelson. Things got rough in a hurry, and MacLeod never graduated.

"Jazz guys hear so much," he observes. "While they were moving onto Coltrane, I was going back to

Jimmy McGriff. The bluesy kind of jazz. Bill Evans. Ahmad Jamal. Hampton Hawes. That's what I listen to. I'm just grateful I don't have to play with them."

His next attempt at musical respectability prompted a move to Los Angeles in 1974. Disregarding his inability to read notation and his considerable struggles at Berklee, MacLeod felt he should try to make a living as a studio musician and that L.A. was the best place to give it a shot.

There were private pressures in play.

"I met my first wife in Boston. A nice gal," he looks back. "She met a friend of mine from the Norfolk days who told her a bunch of stories about me. She didn't want any part of it and I can't say I blame her. My time in Norfolk was, let's say . . . adventurous."

The master plan was to give up the blues for a more peaceful life as a legit, nine-to-five, union dues-paying musician. But like his ill-fated adventures in jazz academia in Boston, his career as a Los Angeles studio player stalled in the starting blocks.

"I still couldn't read music worth a damn. It was pitiful. Once I was at a recording session and the producer, who was really something, came up to me and said, 'Make this sound like a Malibu sunrise.' I'm busy trying to read the fuckin' notes and he's talkin' about a Malibu sunrise."

MacLeod, a skilled mimic, effectively conjures an image of the puffed-up, effeminate, thoroughly displeased tormentor who put him out of work.

"Finally, he asked me if I could play it like Larry Carlton. I got impatient and said, 'Well, if that's how you feel, why don't you hire Larry Carlton?' Everybody in the studio saw that and thought, that's it, he's dead. My studio career ended that day."

The reason MacLeod struggled at Berklee and during his early days in L.A.: He was trying to be something he wasn't. It went against everything Ernest Banks had taught him.

For a while, he hooked on with pop singer Mary MacGregor, whose hit single "Torn Between Two Lovers" had topped the Billboard charts in 1976. The gig was steady enough, but pushed him even further away from his spiritual ground zero in Toano, Virginia. Though years had passed since those afternoons in Banks' kitchen, the blues still held him firmly in its grip.

Early in 1978, while on tour with MacGregor in Dallas, Texas, MacLeod met his soulmate. His "East Texas Sugar." From the start, he could always share his troubles with Patti Joy Wiley, who would soon become his second wife. By now, he had separated from the woman who had moved to Los Angeles with him.

He opened up to Patti Joy about feeling lost. He told her how much he missed the blues.

"She said if that's what I wanted to do, I should try it. When I got back to L.A., I saw an ad in the *LA Weekly* advertising Albert Collins at the Whiskey a Go Go. So I went down there. There was a bottom floor where the audience sat, and I noticed there was something going on upstairs. That's where all the guys were."

Tucking what must have been a considerable amount of jitters into his back pocket, MacLeod followed the trail of musicians to where the action was. The first man he encountered had the streetwise look of a kingpin about him. He wore a tight afro, suit and tie and was right in the middle of things.

"He was walkin' around, meetin' everybody. I heard one of the guys call over to him and then I knew it was Shakey Jake Harris."

Harris, whose nickname derived from his skill at shooting craps, had built a reputation as a first-class singer and harmonica player in Chicago before moving to Los Angeles in the late 1960s. He now ran a popular nightspot called the Safari Club.

"Hey, how you doin' man!" MacLeod does Shakey Jake in a buoyant, raspy voice.

"You're Shakey Jake Harris from Chicago, right?"

"Yeah!" responded the rasp. "Who are you?"

"Doug MacLeod."

"Uh. Doug who?"

"Doug MacLeod. Bass player. St. Louis."

Harris pretended to know him. It's another common courtesy in the bluesman code of etiquette. MacLeod told him he had recently relocated to Los Angeles. Harris asked if he was still playing bass. No, he said, he was a guitar player now.

"You lookin' for work?" asked the rasp.

Doug nodded, and that was it. Harris invited him to come around Shakey Jake's Safari Club at West 54th Street and South Vermont Avenue the following Wednesday night. MacLeod started hanging around there and at the Pioneer Club further south along Vermont, the popular juke joint run by singer-guitarist Smokey Wilson. The roughly thirty blocks between the two nightclubs formed the axis of the city's underground blues scene in the 1970s. Old-school heavyweights played and hung out there – Albert Collins, Pee Wee Crayton, Big Joe Turner – as well as the next wave that included Rod Piazza, William Clarke and Hollywood Fats. MacLeod grabbed every opportunity to show what he could do on guitar.

One night, he had finished his set at Shakey Jake's and was nursing a beer at the bar.

"A fellow came up and told me he liked the way I played. I thanked him and asked him if he also played and what kind of guitar he played." Turns out his admirer wasn't an axeman, but one of the most technically proficient harmonica players the blues has ever known.

"He told me his name was George 'Harmonica' Smith. That's when everything changed. When I met George."

* * *

ON WAX, PART 1:
The Making of *Break The Chain*

Vincent Abbate: Would you like to talk about *Break The Chain*?

Doug MacLeod: I'd love to.

VA: Tell me about the circumstances of the recording. The where, when, who and how.

DM: We did it at Skywalker Sound in Marin County in October of 2016. They allotted three days for the album, which they never do.

VA: Who determines that?

DM: Reference Recordings. The reason they gave us an extra day was that my son Jesse, who sings on the album, was diagnosed with a spindle cell melanoma. This was six months before we did the record.

They book Skywalker maybe seven or eight months in advance. We usually have two days. We go in, there's no overdubs, no pitch control, no mailing in the parts. You do it like they did back in the 30s and the 40s. You might do two or three takes and use the best one.

So, we were all set with the songs when Jesse had this . . . thing. His dentist saw it and told him to have it checked out. They found out he had a spindle cell melanoma cancer. But they didn't know exactly what kind it was. They did a biopsy and it went to UCLA. They kept telling us, "We'll know next week." But the doctors could not find out what it was.

It went to Houston, to their department. We were really concerned. My family was on a roller coaster. The people from the label called and said if we didn't want to do the album, it was fine. My manager Miki said I should just find out what my family wanted. I sat down with Patti Joy and Jesse and asked them what they wanted to do. Within about ten minutes, we decided to do the album.

They still didn't know if Jesse's melanoma had metastasized or gone to the lymph nodes. Nobody knew anything. The doctors had never seen one like it.

So . . . we go and do the album. When you see the pictures of us on the inner sleeve, of everybody who was involved in that record, everybody in that studio knew what was going on with Jesse. We did the record and still hadn't had any word.

Jesse drove home one day before me. When I got home the next night, I got a call from Jesse. He says, "Yeah, it is serious." He told me they were sending his biopsy to Johns Hopkins, because that's the best cancer research center in America.

In the meantime, while we were waiting, Jesse called me and said, Pops, let's go play golf and get some fried clams on the pier. He used to like those fried clams when he was a little boy. I could tell what was going on. He was asking his dad for help. Help in getting over this.

They put him in a cancer treatment center and he felt like he didn't belong in those places, where people are getting chemo. It was scary for him. They cut it out and went even further beyond the margin than usual. They gave him radiation and didn't know if it would affect his voice. It didn't. Then they gave him immunotherapy. It's to make sure it hadn't traveled in his bloodstream.

By the grace of God, he's cancer-free now. We found out he was cancer-free right around Christmas. That was a big Christmas gift. We were so lucky.

My bass player Denny Croy is a cancer survivor, too, and he also has to have it checked all the time. Denny had a serious one. The doctor missed it. They thought it was cat scratch fever. But it was really serious. We were worried if he was gonna make it or not. So Denny did the album with Jesse, knowing Jesse had been diagnosed with cancer. I think he helped Jesse an enormous amount, because he never stopped working. All through the chemo. You could tell he was tired, but Denny kept going. Denny's an incredible human being, besides being one of the best bass players that ever came down the pike.

When we were doing *Break The Chain*, the love and the caring we all felt, the understanding of what life is and how fragile it is and how you don't really know what's happening, even though you think you do . . . that was the mood of that album. When we got done, we knew it was a good record. The hugs, the feelings. There were tears. The love that was there. It was an incredible time.

VA: Let's talk about the songs, starting with something lighter. "Mr. Bloozeman." There and in another song on the album you use the term "popcorn" as an insult. *You're just a popcorn to me.* Where did you get that?

DM: (*laughing*) I guess from one of the old blues guys I was running around with. They would say, like, "That motherfucker a popcorn." You'd look at the guy and think, yeah, popcorn! I don't know what it means, but it sounds great.

VA: I assume you were inspired to write "Mr. Bloozeman" by watching certain musicians at festivals.

DM: Not at festivals. It was inspired by the time Patti Joy and I went to see this local guy play. A harmonica player. He had the bandoleros going across, the two-tone black and white shoes, the hat, the sunglasses. Juke Logan used to use the term "suit, shuffles and shades." When he played, he sounded horrible. Patti looked over at me and said, "I got a name for him. I'm gonna call him Harmonica Pud." So, Harmonica Pud, whoever he was, inspired that song.
I had to write a song about it, because it was pitiful. If somebody is young and this was their introduction to the blues, they would think the blues is a joke.

VA: I figured it was aimed at some of today's bluesrock guitarists.

DM: You mean guys like Walter Trout? No. I know Walter and I know what he plays is real. It's got nothing to do with that. It's the clones. It's like Bruce

Bromberg said. Stevie Ray Vaughan was the best thing and the worst thing for blues. The best thing, because he turned on a whole generation to this music. But he came from that place. Stevie Ray Vaughan could play like Albert King. It's scary. He played it the other way. Albert played it backward, so he could use the bicep to bend the strings. Stevie had to push them up. But these other guys hear him and think that's what they have to play. But they can't play like him.
So the song is really about the Mr. Bloozemen of the world. You know, these guys who play harmonica on Friday and Saturday night and only play in the second position. They don't know how to play in the first or third or fourth, like Musselwhite and Estrin, the real guys.

VA: On that same song, you mention the names of some of your role models. And the solo section, if I'm hearing it correctly, is in the style of Lonnie Johnson. You also devote a whole song to Tampa Red. Could you say a word about each of them and what impact they had on you?

DM: Tampa Red was one of the most melodic slide players that ever came down the pike. Like B.B. King, he could do so much with so little. If you listen to his

style, it's like a voice singing. He would play it and "worry" the notes, as we call it. The tone that he got on his National was just gorgeous. I also think he's one of the best songwriters the blues has ever seen. He's underrated, I think.
And Lonnie Johnson . . . what a hell of a guitar player. He played jazz, he played blues, played in different tunings. And his singing. One of my all-time favorite songs is "Another Night To Cry." Wow. What a guitar solo. What a great voice. I love the video of that. I'm a Lonnie Johnson freak.
There's also a Jimmie Reed quote in my solo on "Mr. Bloozeman."

VA: Was that planned or spontaneous?

DM: A little of both. Actually it was Patti Joy who suggested I make a little claim to the guys that influenced me. That whole solo is an example of less is more.

VA: "This Road I'm Walking" is a really funny one. At the end, Denny starts talking in the background and you cut it off abruptly. What happened there? Did he throw you off?

DM: No! That's how we do our gigs. He says, "It's hard when you're alone." And then I say something like "Sometimes!" It was a live thing. That's how we have fun. So we decided to keep it.

VA: It's a laugh out loud song, but there's a lot of truth in it.

DM: There is. It's the funniest thing. In America, the women don't get that. It's like they're insulted. The one they like to hear is "The Addition To Blues." That was about a woman who wanted to have a one-night stand with me. I told her I was happily married with a young kid, and she said, "I'm not talkin' about instead of, I'm talkin' in addition to." That's the song they like! I asked one lady why she asked for that one. She said it was because it's sexy. I'll never understand women.
Now, the message behind "This Road I'm Walking" is, fellas, you can't keep looking for the perfect woman. It's like that song I wrote with Bruce Bromberg for Billy Lee Riley, "Perfect Woman": If you're looking for the perfect woman, you're gonna die a lonely man. You know?! You got a good gal, 85% . . . be happy with it!

VA: Maybe women don't like it because you use the word "fat."

DM: Bobby Rush told me, never tell a lady she looks fat. Just tell her the dress is too small.

VA: What about "Going Home"?

DM: That one was inspired by Koerner, Ray & Glover. I think it was on the album *Blues, Rags & Hollers*, Dave "Snaker" Ray sings what they call a field holler. When I was thinking about this album, it was Jeff Turmes, who plays with Mavis Staples, who suggested I do a song that features my voice. So, what more could you do to feature your voice than sing a song with nobody else there?
I am a spiritual guy. I don't know if I'm a religious guy. I think religion comes from humans, and spirituality comes from a higher power. That's my belief. But I have been a witness to special things. I do believe in a higher power. And I believe that we are all on a journey home. *If tomorrow finds me gone, just know I'm going home.*
We're all on our way home. And if we all knew how nice home was, we'd wanna leave this place right now. I believe the angels come.

VA: Do you remember when or where you wrote "Going Home"?

DM: It just came one night.

VA: And recording it?

DM: I just stood at the microphone and sang it. It was done in one take. Most of the songs on the album are one take.

VA: The title song, "Break The Chain," is about overcoming abuse. You wrote it together with your son Jesse, right?

DM: Yeah. I sing the first part, and there's a break, then another guitar comes in. That's Jesse. I'm in one tuning, he's in another tuning. I play some slide. And of course we did it live, like we always do. There are no overdubs. He was looking at me. Singing about how the chain of abuse has been broken. For the rest of this lineage of my family, it's over. It's over. It was Jesse's idea to do a song about it.
The first time I played the song live was at a festival in Denmark. It was the kind of place where everybody is standing up. Maybe 350, 400 people. Nobody was sitting down, but they were all listening.

At the very end of my concert, I felt like I was gonna do "Break The Chain." I explained that it was about breaking the chain of abuse in families. I talked about my son and how much it meant to me to break the chain of abuse. And also to forgive. That's the other part. It's the hardest thing – to forgive the people who did it to you.

So while I'm singing it, I'm seeing people move, like the parting of the Red Sea. A young man comes up to the very front and sits down like a Buddhist, with his legs crossed and his hands facing up, and listens to the very end. It was the last song in the set. Afterward, I'm signing CDs, talking to people. It must have taken 40 minutes. He waited. At the very end, he came to me and said, "Mr. MacLeod? It means I still got a chance, don't I?" I said yes, young man, you've got a chance.

That's when I knew that song was going to speak to people. I saw his eyes. I don't know what kind of abuse he suffered, or was suffering, but I knew then how important that song is. Now, I play it at almost every concert. You'd be surprised how many people come up to me to say thanks. A lot of people have gone through it.

VA: Do you want to talk about your own experiences with abuse?

DM: I'm so lucky. Because my life, before, was violent. Most people look at me now and say, oh, he's a sweet guy. But I was violent. I got into relationships that were violent. I sought it out. Because of what happened to me. I didn't know it! It was traumatic. Blacked out in my mind. I knew something was wrong, because I couldn't understand why I would break up with a girl who was really sweet and make her feel terrible and then go to some woman who carried a knife or a gun, some violent relationship.

What changed it was, I fell in love with a girl, and I don't really wanna say any more than that, like who she is, or was. I don't know if she's alive or not. She attempted suicide. And when she attempted suicide, she called and told me she had taken too many pills and was going to die. I asked her where she was. She gave me the name of a hotel and I told her I was coming right over. Before I left, I called the police, who got in touch with emergency, and they saved her.

Then we went to therapy. That's when I found out that the abuse had happened. The doctor told me I had experienced some traumatic events and blacked them out. I didn't realize the scope of it at that time though.

VA: So you only found out then.

DM: Late in my life. I knew something had happened because . . . this is a disgusting story. There was this woman, a friend of my mother, who used to babysit me. She was now living in Beverly Hills. I had separated from my first wife at the time, so my mother called me and suggested I go over to visit this woman for Thanksgiving dinner. I said OK. So I go over there. A nice place. A mansion. Two floors with all these bedrooms. They had the turkey cooking and everything.

The woman, my former babysitter, says to me, "Come on upstairs with me." Then she says to me – this is true – "Do you remember when I played with your peepee and dressed you like a girl? And how much you liked it? Would you like to do that again with me? And maybe with my daughter?"

That knocked me fuckin' out. I thought, *this* is why! And I got out of there as fast as I could. I said, I gotta leave. I gotta get outta here.

After that I started to understand what had happened. My mother was ailing and she was starting to give out some things about my heritage and all these different things she never talked about. I told her about the incident and that my babysitter had abused me when I was a little boy. My mother, bless her heart, said, "No, Doug, she didn't abuse you. Your cousin did." That's how I found out that two people had abused me.

I went back to therapy and told them I needed help. Now I know why I'm so screwed up!

It took me so long to get here. I mean, every day I thank God that he gave me enough time to be sitting here as I am today. That he gave me enough time that I'm finally getting my music together. That I'm making music that talks to people instead of sabotaging things.

So when Jesse said, "Pops, let's do this song" . . . I don't know if he knew the extent of the abuse, but in my family, that doesn't matter. All that matters is the love that we have. That is so powerful. The power of love – when someone loves you – you can break the chain. My son said, "Pops, let's break the chain. Let's let people know that we broke the chain."

* * *

Jesse & Doug MacLeod, 2017.

LAUGHING JUST TO KEEP FROM CRYING

The sexual abuse Doug MacLeod endured as a child became his hidden demon. Because it was visited upon him at so tender an age – while he was just a boy living in North Carolina – he succeeded in blotting it out of his conscious memory for decades. For years, the pain he had buried drove him like the Devil at the wheel of a Cadillac.

Doug doesn't like to reveal many specifics of the bad behavior that was typical of his youth and young adulthood. He talks of himself as having been violent and full of rage. He speaks of darkness, self-sabotage and thoughts of suicide. He admits there were friends who became enemies because of his seething anger and the inability to channel it. At some point, a doctor told him music was his only way out. A safety valve.

"She told me music is my way to handle this. That I should use the music more."

MacLeod will tell you the blues chose him. Not the other way around.

"If I think about my younger days and what happened to me, it's no wonder I gravitated to this music. At first it was probably because I was feeling sorry for myself. Blues, right? But when you get around the musicians and the people and you're actually living in that culture . . . now, there might be some downness, but what they're talking about is living. And laughing. The things that are important. Eat good. Drink good. Live good. Laugh good. Cry good. The basic emotions."

MacLeod has never shied from exploring the dark recesses of his life in song. He has sung about loneliness – *I've tried, Lord knows I've tried/I feel like I don't belong* – and taking the ultimate step to escape it. *Would you miss me if tomorrow find me gone?*

He's written openly about the abuse he suffered in "Come To Find":

I was born in the city, raised up in pain
Abused, confused, confronted with my shame

And, more recently, in the triumphant "Break The Chain":

You've got the power to make a change

You've got the power to stop the pain
You've got the power to break the chain.

Many of his most poignant compositions acknowledge the obstacles every human being faces while offering comfort in the form of hope.

Rise up! Rise up and carry on!
Don't worry about the past,
the past ain't nothing but gone.

The spirit of transcendence also runs through "What The Blues Means To Me," a spoken-word piece from 2017's *Break The Chain* album. Here, he gleans a universal message from his scarred personal history. The blues, he sermonizes, is a music of overcoming adversity, not subjecting to adversity. In that sense, the first blues clubs he visited in St. Louis set the tone for the rest of his life.

"We were in the black part of town, of course," says MacLeod, recalling his nights out with buddy Steve Waldman as an impressionable teenager. "And I saw all these people celebrating life. They were poorer than me. A few generations removed from slavery. And yet there they were, enjoying life, enjoying music, eating good and laughing. I said, wow. I like this. I wanna be around this."

Thanks to those formative experiences and his subsequent escapades in Norfolk, the heady Los Angeles blues scene he entered in the late 1970s felt secure and familiar to him. It was where he wanted to be. Surrounded by blues greats like Joe Turner, Pee Wee Crayton and Lowell Fulson – the men who would ultimately show him the ropes – MacLeod knew he had entered an exclusive sanctuary not generally open to people like himself.

"Those guys accepted me. I don't know why. They sensed something from me. Or I sensed something from them. I felt I belonged there. I felt more comfortable there than I did with my own people. I mean, they laughed and had a good time! My people didn't laugh. My people were always sad, always angry. But those guys were laughing, even though there were troubles. I was glad they said, in so many words: 'You come on with us. You be with us.' From them, I learned how to live my life. How to survive."

Being accepted into that tight inner circle in South L.A. wasn't like joining the Boy Scouts. The musicians MacLeod ran with were a rough-and-tumble, hard-drinking lot, nearly all of them having roots in the Deep South of Texas, Mississippi or Arkansas. More than anything, they were taskmasters on the bandstand. Playing up to their standards was a true rite of passage for the skinny white kid with the kinky hair.

Whenever MacLeod sat in with them, the seasoned vets would cock a critical ear in his direction. If they didn't like what he was doing on guitar, they would get in his face. If MacLeod played too many notes or stepped on anyone's toes, he'd get a stern talking to. Usually, there were a few "motherfuckers" thrown in. The term "motherfucker" carried a lot of weight back then.

"If I was jiving, they would take me in the back and say, 'Motherfucker, don't you play like that again or I'll break your motherfuckin' face.' Now, somebody talks to you like that, you gonna sit up and take notice, right? Especially when you're skinnier than them."

Among the blues men and women who showed him the ropes, MacLeod forged a particularly close bond with Connie Curtis "Pee Wee" Crayton, the Texas-born guitarist who had settled in Los Angeles in the 1940s and scored a number one R&B hit with "Blues After Hours." MacLeod looked up to Crayton like a beloved uncle and felt accepted by him in a way that might seem peculiar to outsiders.

"He always thought there was black blood in me," MacLeod remembers. "I'd get done singing and playing a song and he'd lean over and say something like, 'I knew there was a nigger in the woodpile.' I know the 'N' word is politically incorrect nowadays. But back then if a black blues musician called you a nigger it was a high compliment. Pee Wee told his friends I was the 'white nigger motherfucker' that played guitar for him. High praise indeed."

MacLeod credits Crayton with teaching him how to play with taste.

"He used to always say, 'Take your time.' In fact, on my guitar I had a piece of paper scotched taped to the back that said 'TYT.'

Eventually, Crayton became godfather to MacLeod's first and only child Jesse following his birth in 1984.

His true mentor during this period and his second great teacher after Ernest Banks, however, was George "Harmonica" Smith. The history books claim this somewhat overlooked master of chromatic harp was born in West Helena, Arkansas in 1924, but MacLeod is dubious.

"You know why? Because George would be playing somewhere and a guy would come up to him and say, 'George, you're the best harmonica player I ever heard in my life!' George would say thank you and ask the person where he was from. Let's say the man was born in Alabama. George would say, 'Hey, man, I was born in Alabama!' The guy would say, 'No!

Lemme buy you a drink.' A couple days later he'd be talking to another guy – I'm exaggerating to make a point – and the guy would go, 'George, you're the best harmonica player I ever heard!' George would say thank you and ask him where he was from. Now this guy says Montana. George would tell him he was born in Montana and the guy would buy him a drink! One day we were driving and I asked George where he really was born. He said, 'Dubb, I was born wherever the liquor is coming from.'"

Smith was raised in Illinois and played briefly in the bands of Otis Rush and Muddy Waters before a 1955 tour with Champion Jack Dupree deposited him on the left coast. He recorded sporadically throughout the 1960s and 1970s and had already mentored young harp protégés like Rod Piazza and William Clarke before running into Doug MacLeod at Shakey Jake's Safari Club.

When their paths first crossed, Doug had already made up his mind to write and play his own music. He was grateful for the chance to sit in with the legends, and did so whenever he could, but he saw no sense in trying to copy them.

"I didn't want to sing 'Got My Mojo Workin'' and all these old chestnuts, because there's no way I'm going to sing 'Mojo Workin'' and make you forget about Muddy Waters. Or 'The Thrill Is Gone.' Please. I got no business doing those things."

Smith, more than 20 years his senior, admired his commitment and gladly took the newcomer under his wing. Often, he would come down and join MacLeod on the Redondo Beach Pier, where the guitarist was appearing with his own combo. And because Smith was well-connected, others – like Crayton, Lowell Fulson and Big Mama Thornton – followed.

"We started to make a little noise," says MacLeod of the earliest incarnations of his Los Angeles-based electric band. There's a certain sentimentality in the telling – an accomplished professional smiling upon his musical infancy – though he admits money was tight.

"I had an unemployment check for 250 dollars a month. That covered the little duplex Patti Joy and I lived in. She was working as a waitress and somehow we were just getting by. For me, it was about writing and creating music."

Smith would use him on guitar for local gigs and began taking him out on tour as well. He even punched MacLeod's first ticket to Europe when, in 1981, the harmonica player was booked to play a series of dates in Sweden. Smith had sent a promo still to his Swedish promoter prior to the tour.

MacLeod – plain as day in the photo – was the only white member of the band. Reverse discrimination, as ugly as it was unexpected, brought the two men even closer.

"I was at George's house when the promoter called," MacLeod remembers. "What he told George was, 'I got the picture, I love the music, but you got a white guy in the band.' He told George he would have to get rid of me and hire a black guy. George said, 'Well, when you heard the music, you weren't concerned about it. Why are you concerned about it now?' The guy told him he couldn't sell a white guy out front of his band."

Smith held firm. No Dubb, no George. The tour went off as planned.

"The love he showed me and the love I had for him will never die. I learned so much from him. Great lessons. Father-type lessons. I think it's because of him that I've got a career."

Though MacLeod would hold down a regular gig on the Redondo Beach Pier throughout the 1980s, Smith suggested early on that playing electric blues in a band setting might not be where his true talent lies. Like MacLeod, his elder companion had a soft spot for the folksy, front porch blues of Big Bill Broonzy.

"Once, we had just got done with a show. He came up to me and said, 'Dubb, you sure do sound like B.B. King.' I thanked him, and he said, 'Dubb, that's not a compliment.'"

Like Ernest Banks before him, Smith was telling MacLeod to be himself.

"I was a good electric player. But I didn't really feel comfortable with bands. I'm much more comfortable when it's just me, my right hand, my left hand and my foot. Just sitting alone onstage, even at a festival, I have so much confidence in what all this" – he wiggles his fingers – "can do. It's sort of a unique sound. And I think George knew that."

Smith, who passed away in 1983, didn't stick around long enough to see MacLeod step out on his own and become the acoustic performer he is today. But if he is indeed watching from above, as his friend believes, he'll notice a career trajectory eerily similar to the one he predicted.

"Today, the blues audience is predominantly white," observes MacLeod. "Back when I started, it was predominantly black. I remember George telling me, 'Dubb, my people get you. My people know you. But it's gonna take a long time for your people to get you.' And it's kind of played out that way, hasn't it? I mean, I've got my fault in it, because of what I did to sabotage my life. But it has turned out that way."

* * *

If you press him, MacLeod admits he doesn't care for much of what passes for blues nowadays. While working as a radio disc jockey in Los Angeles in the 1990s and into the aughts, he stubbornly refused to devote airtime to the over-the-top soloing he refers to as "diarrhea guitar." (A term he copped from Pee Wee Crayton.)

Typically, though, there is empathy in his criticism.

"I think what's happening is that a lot of guys are playing for the audience," he surmises. "What I mean is, they want the audience to respond and to do that, they play a lot of notes. A cascade of notes. And audiences respond. If you're coming from a place where you are needy, if they're giving that love to you – what you consider to be love – then you do that. 'This is where I get it, so this is what I'm gonna do.' If that's the case with some of these musicians, then they should listen to what Luther Allison said: 'Leave your ego, play the music, love the people.' That's what it's about."

The teachers he had in Los Angeles would have knocked that me-first attitude right out of him.

"I remember the first time I played with George. I was driving back to the little apartment Patti and I had, and I remember telling her, 'I gotta be around this guy. Because when the gravy falls off that plate, I want it to fall on me. I wanna get some of this.' Because I saw him care about people. It wasn't him first. It was the audience first. He gave to them, they gave back to him and things just went higher and higher."

MacLeod appreciated how established blues musicians like Albert Collins, Lowell Fulson and Big Joe Turner would never dream of referring to themselves as artists.

"They called themselves entertainers. Because being an artist meant you were more important than someone else. But the education I got from the old bluesmen was, yeah, you can play guitar and you can sing and the girls like you. Can you fix the under-the-floor plumbing? No. Can you fix your car? No. Can you build a room on the end of your house? No. So are you more special than the guys who can? No. That's your gift. The mechanic gives his gift so your car runs good. The plumber gives his gift so the plumbing runs good. And if everybody gave their gift to the best of their ability, this old world would turn around pretty good, wouldn't it?

"The wisdom those guys had – the ones that I ran with – came through in their music and it came through in their entertaining."

MacLeod's troubles weren't forgotten then and they are by no means forgotten today, even as life, on the surface, has grown progressively more comfortable for him. But the blues, at the very least, gave him a foothold when he most needed it. The scared stutterer was left cowering somewhere in the past. In Los Angeles, MacLeod bonded with men who came from far less privileged environments than the one he had grown up in. His father didn't like it any more than his nightly wanderings in St. Louis. But he was living his own life now, married for the second time, a professional musician, his first child on the way. Even if there wasn't much left over at the end of the month, he was surviving.

"I think the most important thing I learned from my time associating and traveling with black people and doing our thing was, there might not have been a lot of money, but you could eat good, love good, drink good. If you have all that and have somebody who cares about you – my goodness – you're a pretty rich person."

* * *

PHOTO GALLERY

Dubb, age one.

On bass (center) with The Fliptones, ca. 1960.

Norfolk, Virginia, ca. 1965.

At the Folk Ghetto, Norfolk, VA, 1966.

With Beau Johnson (r.), Virginia Beach, 1967.

With Eddie Ahearn (l.) & George "Harmonica" Smith (c.),
ca. 1978.

With Lloyd Glenn, Stockholm, ca. 1982.

Jamming with Pee Wee (c.) and Marshall Crayton (r.), ca. 1985.

Hanging with The Hook.

With John "Juke" Logan, 1999.

With Robert Lockwood Jr.

With Bobby Rush (l.) & Otis Clay (r.).

George.

THERE GOES MY HERO

(*Author's note*: Onstage and off, Doug MacLeod loves to tell a story. Having traveled the world playing the blues for over a half century, he has crossed paths with more than a few musical legends. In this section, highlighting some of the most notable encounters, the words are his. – VA)

"YOU'RE UP HERE WITH ME"

I already told you about when I backed up Chuck Berry in St. Louis, right?

Well . . . two years later maybe, I'm in the navy and I'm flying home on leave. I'm going from Norfolk to D.C. and then D.C. to St. Louis. On a TWA jet. Like he sang about in that song "Brown Eyed Handsome Man." When I get on the plane in D.C. and I'm walking to my seat at the back, I notice that Chuck Berry is in the first-class area. I had my uniform on, and after we took off, I asked the stewardess if it was OK to go and say hello to a gentleman up there in the front. She told me it was okay, but I couldn't stay there.

"No, I just wanna say hello to him."

I guess because I had my uniform on, it was fine. I walked up there and introduced myself and told him I had backed him up at a teen hop at Mosley Electronics in St. Louis.

"I remember that!"

I don't think he did. I said: "That was a real nice night."

He said: "Yeah, it was. What are you doin' now?"

"I'm in the Navy."

"You going home?"

I said, "Yeah, I'm going home for leave."

"Where are you sittin'?"

"I'm in the back."

"Not anymore. You're up here with me."

I sat in first class with Chuck Berry all the way to St. Louis. On a TWA jet. So if you hear some stories about him being such and such a way, well . . . he might've been. But to me? I look back to my experiences with these guys, guys like Robert Lockwood, who was supposed to be such and such. They've all been great. Chuck Berry? Fine.

* * *

"YOU AIN'T SHIT"

George "Harmonica" Smith was involved in this one.

George told me one time, "Dubb, someday you're gonna run into Albert King."

Albert had already done a song of mine. He recorded "Your Bread Ain't Done." I told George about that. He just repeated what he said before.

"One of these days you're gonna run into Albert King."

I told George that Albert had been an idol of mine back in St. Louis. He repeated himself again.

"One of these days you're gonna run into Albert King."

"What's your point, George?"

"He ain't gonna like you."

"What? I wrote a song for him!"

"Listen. He ain't gonna like you. So, all you say to Albert King is 'Thank you, Mr. King.' No matter what he says to you. You say, 'Thank you, Mr. King.'"

I had my band back in those days. We were doing this little cruise in Long Beach Harbor. Albert was the main act and we were the opening act. I was all excited, because I'd seen him as a kid in St. Louis and now I'm gonna be right there with him.

We go down there and we do our show. I'm coming back up to the dressing room area. We were on this ship, right, and there were no partitions. So Albert's area was off to the left and mine was off to the right. We could see each other, but there was room between us. There was a little bit of privacy if you wanted to change.

So I'm walking up there after the set. Albert King calls over.

"Hey!"

I turn around and he goes, "You ain't shit."

I said, "Thank you, Mr. King."

He looks at me like . . . *huh*?

So he goes back down and does his show. But I'm crushed. This is an idol of mine. He did a song of mine. Goddamn, how could that happen?

He came back up after his show and went back into his area. I took my guitar and went back on down. Nothin'. He didn't even look at me. I went down and did another set. We had a good show. I go back. Nothin'. I told myself as I was packing up: You know, you're gonna have days like this.

As I'm walking back down the steps carrying my guitar, Albert calls out to me. "Hey!"

I look over.

He says, "You okay."

I said, "Thank you, Mr. King" and kept walking. He must have been looking at me thinking, "That's one crazy white boy."

About six months later, Albert is back in the Los Angeles area playing at the old Music Machine on Pico Boulevard. I go to see him. He had a guy in front of the door of the dressing room – his personal bouncer. I introduced myself.

"Does Albert know you?"

"Just tell him I wrote the song 'Your Bread Ain't Done.'"

The bouncer goes back to check with Albert, comes back and invites me in.

So I sit down with Albert.

"So you wrote 'Your Bread Ain't Done'? That's a damn good song."

I said, "Thank you, Mr. King."

He looks at me and goes, "Was that *you*?"

* * *

"I MAKE A LOT MORE MISTAKES THAN I USED TO"

I got a good right hand. Honeyboy Edwards had a good right hand. Spider John Koerner had one of the greatest right hands I ever heard in my life. You got Jerry Reed, Big Bill Broonzy and Spider John Koerner.

I was visiting my manager Miki in Minneapolis, which is where Spider John is from. I was there for a gig and we got to talkin', you know? I asked her, "Miki, by any chance do you know Spider John Koerner?" She says, "Yes I do." I say, "No, you don't!" She said, "Yes, I'll give him a call." She called him up and told him I was a real big fan of his and that I would love to meet him.

Well, he's a real cantankerous guy, I guess, but

he said OK and agreed to meet me at Palmer's Bar the next morning. Mind you, this was on a Sunday morning at 10 o'clock.

So I drive down there to meet him. Palmer's is a real joint, but the people are nice. There are a couple of lushes at the end of the bar. The bartender asks me if I want anything. I order a soda water and lime. I tell him I'm there to meet a fellow named Spider John Koerner. "Is he around?"

The bartender tells me I had just passed him.

I look back and say to myself, holy smoke, I think that's him. So I go back and say, "Uh . . . Spider John Koerner?"

He goes: "Yeah."

I introduced myself and he told me to have a seat. We got to talking and I told him how much he had influenced me. He kinda lit up when I said that.

Later on, I found out he was not someone who would talk too much about music. While we were talking I kind of pointed to his right hand and said, "That's a bad right hand right there."

He said, "Well . . . yeah, it was. Now it isn't quite the same. But there's good news and bad news. The bad news is I make a lot more mistakes than I used to. The good news is the audience don't know it."

We spoke about National Guitars. He probably still doesn't know what I do. He probably thought I was just someone who came by the bar. I asked him how he got his sound on the National. He told me, "I doubled it."

I didn't know what he meant. It meant he had two G strings on it. So it was a seven-string guitar. But instead of like a George Van Eps seven-string, where the bass is the seventh string, he added the seventh string on the G string. So when you listen to *Blues, Rags & Hollers* by Koerner, Ray & Glover and you hear him with that rhythm . . . it reminded me of what Ernest Banks told me. You gotta sound like you're more than one guy up there. You gotta have it all going on.

It was great to meet him. Spider John Koerner. A killer right hand. Honeyboy and I would talk about right hands.

Ernest Banks told me, "Your left hand is your brain." If you see me play and you know I'm in Bastard G tuning and you look at my left hand, then you'll know what I'm doing. Which chords I'm playing. But what I'm doing with my right hand: That's my personality. That's why, in acoustic blues, Blind Willie Johnson don't sound like Blind Willie McTell who don't sound like Big Bill Broonzy who don't sound like Blind Boy Fuller who don't sound like Son House who don't sound like Lemon Jefferson. The right hands were different.

Sometimes nowadays, with all the electronic stuff, it's hard to tell who it is playing. But those old guys, when you heard them play, you knew exactly who it was.

* * *

"DO YOU ALSO PLAY?"

I first met B.B. King at the L.A. airport when he came in to do that TV show *Sanford & Son.* This was probably around 1977. I was working with Mary McGregor and still married to my first wife. Back in those days, the guitars still came down on the belts. So, my guitar came down and I opened up the case to make sure it was alright. Behind my back, I heard a voice.

"Boy, that's a nice looking guitar."

I looked up at the guy and said thanks. He kind of looked familiar to me.

I asked him, "Do you also play?"

"Yeah, I play a little. You might have heard of me. My name's B.B. King."

"B.B. King! I didn't recognize you. I remember seeing you in St. Louis and Norfolk. You were a little thinner and the hair was different."

"Well." B.B. put his hand on his belly. "Things have been good."

So that was the first time I met The King. Then one time, when I was playing that little bar on Redondo Pier, I noticed that B.B. King was coming in to play at Concerts by the Sea. I think it was Wednesday through Saturday. I figured I'd go down on Wednesday night and meet him. Or at least hear him. I was sitting there listening to him play, thinking how much I loved this guy.

Like he always did, he signed autographs until the last person had gone. I had a business card for my band, The Doug MacLeod Band. I gave it to B.B. to sign. He saw it was a band card, so he asked me if I play. He signed the back of the card: *To Douglas. Stay With It. B.B. King.*

Many years later, in 2008, I got a call to open for him in Seattle. I was amazed. I went up there and did my show. They said 35 minutes. I made sure it was 35 minutes. Know what I mean? It was probably 34. I made sure!

I got off, went back to the dressing room. B.B. was playing, so I got to hear some of him. Then I got ready to head back to the hotel. I changed clothes, got my guitar, and as I was going out, one of B.B.'s guys called out, "Doug! Where you goin'? B.B. wants to meet you." He wants to meet *me*? I'd been carrying that autographed card in my wallet all this time.

This guy hustles me down to the bus, because by now, they were getting ready to leave. He hustles me down there. And I'm waiting. Then I finally get on the bus. B.B.'s bodyguard is there. I'm listening to the music.

I said: "That sounds like Kenny Burrell."

The bodyguard said, "Yeah, that's right."

I said, "That's Kenny Burrell and Jimmy Smith, *Blue Bash!*"

He goes, "Yeah! You like that music?" I told him I was a big fan of Kenny Burrell. He said B.B. was a big Kenny Burrell fan.

While I'm waiting, I'm like this kid. I must have been 60 years old, but I'm like a kid. I'm thinking about that little card in my back pocket. Finally, I get escorted into the bus to meet B.B. He says he likes how I play. I tell him he's an idol of mine. I start gushing. Everybody around could see I was gushing.

"Mr. King, can I show you something?"

"Yeah."

"You know, back in 1981, you signed this card for me. And you said to stay with it. Well, I have stayed with it. And finally, here I am with you."

He looks carefully at the card and goes: "That's not my signature."

I nearly died. Everybody in the back of that bus started laughing. And then I saw B.B. grin. Oh no! I've been had by The King!

We laughed and so on and he wished me the best. And that was the last time I saw him.

It reminds me of the time I saw him in Schiphol Airport in Amsterdam. He had one of those baggage carts, you know? He had his bags on there and he was carrying his guitar, Lucille. He's rolling it along. I was tired. I was beat. It was one of those times in this business where you're traveling all the time and there's no rest. I saw him a ways off and I said to myself, Douglas MacLeod, you better shut up, because if The King is doing that, then this little serf better be doing it, too. Without complaining. It's like that old saying: You've got a choice of working two ways. You can either work gratefully or you can work grudgingly. I choose gratefully.

* * *

"To Douglas. Stay With It. B.B. King"

ON WAX, PART 2:
Some Old Blues Song

And the winner is . . .

Lately, Doug MacLeod's name has been appearing more frequently at the end of that particular sentence. Since 2014, when he finally took home his first Blues Music Award at the age of 68 – he'd been nominated many times before – the Memphis-based Blues Foundation and its members have regularly recognized MacLeod's music at the award gathering held there each spring. He was a two-time winner that first year, claiming victory in the Best Acoustic Artist category and for his album *There's A Time*. He was again chosen Best Acoustic Artist in 2016 and 2017. Most recently, *Break The Chain* was celebrated as Acoustic Album of the Year – a particularly meaningful honor considering the circumstances of the recording and the subject matter underlying the title track.

"I remember the first time they called my name. I heard it and thought, holy shit, that's me," laughs MacLeod, remembering the 2014 awards ceremony at the Cook Convention Center. "I even said it out loud. There was a young gal next to me and I apologized for swearing in front of her. Then I went up there and told everybody how I never thought I'd be holding one of those trophies. It was as big a moment for me as when Albert Collins did a song of mine or Albert King did a song of mine. It meant a lot to me and it still does."

Of course, MacLeod hasn't always been the toast of the industry. His loyal fan base – affectionately known as DubbHeads – is a fairly recent development. There were plenty of lean years and false starts before his career truly began to pick up speed. George "Harmonica" Smith's prescient comment about how it was going to take a while for Doug's people (i.e. white listeners) to appreciate him proved true. As MacLeod freely admits, he needed time to find himself, both musically and personally.

Following his entry onto the club scene in Los Angeles in the late 1970s, he settled into a comfortable groove as a sideman to the elder statesman and the leader of his own electric band. "I would switch back and forth," he recalls. "I would play locally and go out on tour with George."

Together with bassist Gilbert Hansen and drummer Sam Canzona, he accompanied his harmonica-playing mentor in a four-piece unit Smith loosely referred to as the Gravy Bros. Band. "I think it's because George pronounced Gilbert's name as Giblet," he recalls. "So he was Giblet Gravy. Sam was Italian Gravy. I was White Gravy. I called George Ham Gravy."

At the same time, MacLeod was working to develop his original songs at the bars along the Redondo Beach Pier. The quartet first known as The El Segundo Funk and Rhythm Band eventually morphed into the Doug MacLeod Band, which featured Doug on guitar and vocals, Eric Ajaye on bass, Lee Spath on drums and a roster of ever-changing piano players. Back then, he remembers, you could go out to hear live music seven nights a week along the beaches in Los Angeles. He was a steady presence there throughout the 1980s and into the 1990s.

"We had eleven years playing all original music in Redondo Beach. We weren't making grand theft money, but we were doing alright. I was paying my guys much more than scale," says MacLeod, proud of the fact. He and his band recorded four albums of electric blues between 1984 and 1991, culminating in *Ain't The Blues Evil.* The stylized cover of that LP shows MacLeod reclining on a bed with a Fender Stratocaster, legs crossed, his eyes staring coldly into space. You can't help wonder if his label people were hoping to emulate the look of successful 1980s blues acts like Stevie Ray Vaughan or the Fabulous Thunderbirds.

The sepia photograph gracing the front of his next release *Come To Find*, which appeared in 1994, suggest a significant transformation had taken place. For one, an acoustic guitar has replaced MacLeod's electric model. His right arm is draped atop its wooden corpus the way a loving dad would shield his child from danger. He gazes directly into the camera, his head cocked at an unthreatening angle. His facial expression is fairly neutral, still rather serious, but there is unquestionably the trace of a smile in there.

Come To Find marked the beginning of MacLeod's transformation into the acoustic bluesman he is today.

"I felt myself being pulled back to my roots. Pulled back to that old man I met in Virginia," he explained, looking back roughly a decade later. "I remember telling my wife, 'I think I wanna go acoustic.' She said, 'Well, go.'" But MacLeod was leery. There didn't appear to be much opportunity for an acoustic bluesman in Los Angeles. He was already earning a decent living with his electric band. Patti Joy, as always, encouraged him. "She said if that's what's in your heart, do it. So that's how it happened. I just stopped one day."

The song he wrote about taking the leap of faith gave his subsequent album *Unmarked Road* its name.

"I wrote that song about doing something and all of a sudden, you realize you don't wanna spend the rest of your life doing that. Even though you're going to take chances or you might miss things, it's a scary thing. But you know you gotta get on that unmarked road. Get on it and go. So far – knock on wood – it's turned out to be a really good decision."

One reviewer, commenting on 1997's *Unmarked Road*, felt MacLeod's "dark singing and sparse guitar" were a throwback to the country blues of the 1930s. He found the songs "haunting and mildly disturbing" and was left with the feeling that "there is a great deal beneath the surface."

The attributes that online scribe responded to are indeed key elements of the music MacLeod has been recording and performing since his heart-driven decision to change direction some 25 years ago. The catalog of several hundred songs he has compiled by now contains some that are brooding, others that are humorous, many that are autobiographical. By design, every one of them should mean something to the listener.

"I like to think my songs send a message about how to get through this life. I've always thought this music – the blues – is about that. A lot of people will tell you it's about getting drunk, having a party, and there is some of that. But what I got out of this music is *surviving.* I've listened to this music and found these messages. Like *the way I loved you is the way I hate you now.* Ain't that the truth! When you break up with someone, or someone breaks up with you. It sounds so simple, but it comes with so much weight."

At his live shows, MacLeod likes to tell audiences that the pioneering country bluesman who inspired him – Tampa Red, Big Bill Broonzy, Blind Willie McTell – were very much what we today call singer/songwriters. Far from recycling blues clichés, those first and second-generation troubadours wrote from experience and filled their songs with the vivid imagery of their everyday toils and adventures. MacLeod endeavors to do the same.

At the songwriting workshops he periodically conducts, he offers students a word of advice. "I tell them not to edit until they are done. Let the song come." And when it comes, day or night, the songwriter's duty, as he sees it, is to nail it down.

"If something comes to me and I'm exhausted, you know, maybe I'm lying in a nice bed in a beautiful B&B in the English countryside when that song comes. If I say no? Well, then I know Chris Smither is gonna get it, because the song will go over to Chris Smither. 'Chris, wake up, MacLeod didn't want this one. You want it?'"

Yet while he takes his lyrical cue from some of the great country blues artists of the past, he is quick to point out the differences in his musical style. It's easy to see him sitting onstage with one of his National resonator guitars, stomping his foot, fingerpicking or using the slide and draw comparisons with Blind Boy Fuller or Bukka White. Too easy.

"My style of acoustic blues is not what the old guys played," he stresses. "I'm using octaves. They are what I call 'George Benson' octaves, with a fourth in the middle. And I get my right hand grooves from Jimmy McGriff, the Hammond B3 player."

His hardcore passion for jazz shows up again and again in his phrasing.

"If you're a guitar player, chances are all you listen to is guitar players. Sometimes that gets a little stale. So you gotta listen to someone else who's playing another instrument." In MacLeod's case, listening to wind players has caused him to prefer an economical style.

"Harmonica players. Saxophone players.

Trumpet players. They all literally have to breathe. Or Coltrane. With all the notes he was playing, he was breathing. He wasn't some guitar player sitting there and shredding."

Consequently, MacLeod doesn't just trot out hundred-year-old conventions when he plays. He invigorates the country blues tradition by incorporating all his musical influences. Listeners with more conservative leanings have noticed this and occasionally given him shit about it.

"I met this one blues Nazi who said to me, just because I was playing octaves the way I do: 'Robert Johnson would have never done that.' You're gonna tell me that if Robert Johnson had heard Wes Montgomery, he wouldn't wanna play like that?' If he had lived longer, he might have beaten Wes to it!"

* * *

By rough count, Doug MacLeod has written around 400 songs in the past 50 years. He claims to remember every one of them. But he is loath to pick out favorites. It's like asking a parent to choose his favorite child.

One of a handful of BMA-nominated songs, "Dubb's Talkin' Politician Blues," from his 2005 release *Dubb*, is a crowd-pleasing monologue set to a lightly swinging groove. There's a good chance he picked up that rhythm listening to Louis Jordan coming from the neighbor's house as a boy. Lyrically, the song takes a common-man swipe at two-faced, con artist policymakers. Laced with bitter irony, it's a vehicle for MacLeod's undeterred humor.

"Anything that makes people laugh. Makes 'em feel good."

When he performs "The Entitled Few," an exceptional cut from 2013's *There's A Time*, the mood turns dead serious. With his foot tap-tap-tapping like the incessant rain in John Lee Hooker's Tupelo, MacLeod airs a litany of grievances against callous members of the privileged class.

He recalls the incident that inspired the song's first verse.

"I was going out to eat with a friend who works in the entertainment industry in Hollywood. A wealthy guy. He couldn't find a parking spot and got all frustrated and angry. So he pulled into the blue handicapped spot and pulled out the placard to show he was handicapped. I said, 'I didn't know you were handicapped.' He said, 'I'm not. This thing cost me 5000 dollars.' I went along and had dinner with him. But it's the last time we ever saw each other. That was it. The friendship was over."

The song's ghostly final verse speaks to the

equality of death.

"The one time you won't be one of the entitled few is when Death calls your name. When Death calls and you go, 'Well I don't wanna go yet," Death is gonna say, 'No. You're comin' with me.' That's it."

Every Doug MacLeod concert and every album contains a little of this and a little of that. He juxtaposes humor and social commentary with moments of almost unbearable tension. There are tales of bygone lovers and tributes to musical heroes. There are songs of survival, like the recent "Travel On" – "That's about movin' on from hard times, like what we were going through when Jesse was dealing with his cancer" – and ruminations on the nature of life and God, like his landmark "Where You'll Find Me."

"That's about the spiritual power. The creator. The one that made it possible for you to be alive. If you can find that spot inside of you, and accept that this is you, I think that's where you find peace."

What you won't find on any album or hear at his shows is a cover song. There are just two exceptions, dating back to his *Come To Find* album: "Bring It On Home" and "Rollin' And Tumblin'."

"When I went back to my acoustic roots on *Come To Find*, I wanted to pay tribute to my first harmonica player and pal Beau Johnson. Those were two of our favorite songs to play together."

But MacLeod prides himself on playing original music. If an audience member insists on hearing "Sweet Home Chicago," it comes at a price. MacLeod expects him to make a deposit in what he calls the "Ducat Bucket." It's not allowed to make a sound. Folding money only.

The song that ties everything together – one with which he often closes his shows – is "Some Old Blues Song (aka I Can Count On My Blues)." In its yearning, plainly human lines and elegantly simple refrain – *It ain't nothin' but the blues/There's so damn much that the blues can do* – MacLeod realizes his most poignant expression of gratitude and wonder at the nature of the blues itself.

"Think about the first blues song that touched you," he says as he introduces it to audiences. "The first blues song that actually changed your life. You don't have to call its name. Just think about it. Think about how that song came from a different culture, maybe a different country all across this big ocean and all of a sudden, it reaches you. And the person who's singing it probably wasn't the same color as you. Think about that while I'm singing this song."

He offers "Some Old Blues Song" as a thank you note from a man once adrift at sea, now safe ashore, to the music that rescued him.

"It expresses how much I love this music," says MacLeod earnestly.

Then, accentuating each word:

"I love this music."

* * *

DOUG MacLEOD's DESERT ISLAND DISCS

Born Under A Bad Sign – Albert King

Blues - The Common Ground – Kenny Burrell

Tampa Red - The Guitar Wizard – Tampa Red

The Best of Jimmy Reed – Jimmy Reed

Live At The Regal – B.B. King

The Young Big Bill Broonzy (1928-1935) – Big Bill Broonzy

Howlin' Wolf (aka The Rockin' Chair Album) – Howlin' Wolf

The Real Folk Blues – Sonny Boy Williamson

The Essential Jerry Butler – Jerry Butler

The Worm – Jimmy McGriff

THE YEARS OF LIVING DANGEROUSLY

The blues should be wild, reckless, raw, kinky, intoxicated, edgy and dangerous. Shouldn't it? At least part of the time?

When did the blues – a music sprung from barrelhouses and juke joints, where whiskey flowed, skirts were hiked and punch-ups were the order of the day – become the place where you could pull up a lounge chair and casually grab a beer from the cooler?

Today, the sound of the blues fills casinos, ballrooms and cruise ships where patrons sip cocktails on the pool deck before retiring to cabins that have set them back a couple of grand. Blues shows have become, by and large, a safe, friendly and staid environment. And that's okay. There's little reason to romanticize the knife fights and buckets of blood of days gone by.

Yet it's hard not to feel that previous generations witnessed a more genuine form of the blues that was less a style or uniform than it was a way of life.

"Back in the day, when I was comin' up, if you were 20 years old and you were singing the blues in coffeehouses, you had to be credible," says Doug MacLeod, recalling the years he was stationed in Norfolk, Virginia. He has already admitted to dressing down and intentionally defiling his guitar case in order to look the part. Surely there was more to it than that.

"What I mean is, you had to have some kind of rough life. You couldn't be some guy from middle-class St. Louis, Missouri that joined the Navy and be out there singing the blues. You had to live something, so that the audience would look at you and go, oh yeah, you see that chick he's been running around with? That way, you could feel credible."

MacLeod's stint at the Naval Station Norfolk was easily the wildest period of his life. He was still in his late teens when he arrived, lived off base like most of his fellow sailors and had a regimented job at the radar repair shop that left him ample time for trouble in the evening and on weekends. In seedy

Norfolk, nicknamed the "Armpit of the East Coast" (or, in harsh naval parlance, "Shit City"), there was plenty of trouble to get into.

This was the mid-1960s. The psychedelic movement was in full swing and hallucinogens were en vogue. MacLeod did experiment with drugs, but considering the climate of the times, his indulgences were fairly tame.

"We did do hash," he says, meaning he and his Navy buddies. "There was this one guy who got us this real good hash. And we'd field strip it, like, half a Pall Mall, the tobacco, and then we'd put the hash in it, tighten it up and smoke it. It was OK. Then once, at a party, I tried this very special grass. And man, I remember it was wintertime, and I was looking out of this apartment and there were these branches – just empty branches with no leaves. And I'm saying to myself, 'I should be thinking of something creative.' But the only thing I had on my mind was Chinese food. So I left the party and went and got Chinese!"

MacLeod drew the line at hash, weed and egg rolls, but might have gone further were it not for the intervention of his musical mentor Ernest Banks.

"We used to drink Chianti," MacLeod smiles. "But cocaine was going around. You could get cocaine. I think a lot of it was because of that song Dave Van Ronk made, 'Cocaine Blues.' But hippies, young people . . . we had no idea what this shit was. I mean, I didn't. So I asked Ernest about it.

'What you want that for, boy?'

I told him it was for my music. My playing.

'Why you wanna be a slave, boy?'

I told him I just wanted to try cocaine.

He said, 'You do the cocaine, then you a slave.'

This is a man who wasn't far removed from slavery telling me that's what the drug would do. When you hear a man who knows about slavery tell you that, it kind of turns you away from that drug. I know that's why I never fucked with it. Because of him, I never got into cocaine, heroin, none of that. I never wanted to be a slave."

He wasn't nearly as judicious in his choice of sexual partners.

"I was foolin' around with a couple of prostitutes."

Obviously, in a city teeming with young, randy servicemen, working girls were hardly a rare commodity. MacLeod fell in love with at least one of them – the subject of "Nightbird," a song later brought to perfection by nightclub singer Eva Cassidy.

"But there was another one. I'm not gonna call her name. She was the roughest, toughest woman I ever knew. If she knew where the bed was where she was gonna be workin', she would put a razor blade between the mattresses so she could protect herself. She knew how to handle a knife. She was a rough gal. But good lookin'! It was really nice to be with her, you know?"

The sex was satisfying. On the periphery, the guns, knives and dealing he saw gave him pause. Doug's lady friend ran with a decidedly rough crowd.

"At the same time I was playing in these coffeehouses for the hippie chicks. They were always so sweet and kind. So I thought it might be nice to get a hippie chick on the side. I figured: How are those two worlds ever gonna meet? It's impossible. So I started fooling around on the side. I got something going with one of those hippie girls."

MacLeod knew he was playing with fire. His tough, knife-toting lady was not to be messed with.

"One night I was with her. We got done making love. She started nibbling on my ear. I thought she wanted to go again. I was at the age where I could! But while she's nibbling on my ear, she says, 'Baby, I wanna tell you somethin'. If I ever catch you with another woman, I'm gonna make sure that no other woman wants to have you.'

My stutter came out real big.

'W-w-w-w-what you talkin' about?'

She says, 'I just want you to know that.'

I was really scared. Because she used to break into my apartment. I used to keep Pabst Blue Ribbon quart bottles across the headboard of my bed. And some nights I would put beer cans in the bathtub because you could come through the window there. I did that so that if she was comin' in, I would know. I also had a baseball bat. I was scared."

Sharing the apartment with MacLeod was a New York transplant named Jimmy Sweezy. A fellow sailor who would actually go out on maneuvers from time to time, 'Sweeze' would come and go as he pleased, confident that the key to the apartment would always be waiting for him under the doormat.

"But I didn't want this girl coming in," continues MacLeod. "Sweeze comes home this one time and can't get into the apartment. So he tries to get in through the bathroom window. He's been drinkin'. It's like three in the morning. And of course he steps right into all the empty beer cans in the bathtub."

When MacLeod heard the crunch of aluminum on porcelain, alarm signals sounded. He leapt out of bed and grabbed his baseball bat, ready to defend himself from the crazed hooker who wanted to cut off his private parts.

"I swung the bat just as Sweeze was coming through the door. And I hit the door jamb. Sweeze fell down yelling, 'Mac, it's me, Sweeze!' I was so sorry. I almost killed the guy. This is how nervous that woman made me."

Soon thereafter, MacLeod was getting ready to play one of his coffeehouse gigs in Norfolk. He was so scared his knees were shaking. A fellow folk singer – a wacko who got high on Robitussin cough syrup – noticed and asked him what was wrong.

"Look, man. I'm scared to death."

"It's that woman you got, isn't it?"

"Yeah."

"I got something for you."

Doug thought his acquaintance was going to produce a gun or a knife from his pocket, something he could use to protect himself.

"He reaches into his little pouch – you know how the hippies had these pouches? – and pulls out a bone. It looked like a chicken bone with stripes on it. I asked him what the hell it was.

'Just make a wish on this, man.'

I was so scared I said okay. I said to myself, I hope I never see that girl again. Ever. And I handed him back his bone."

Ten minutes later, MacLeod was preparing to start his set when his worst nightmare appeared outside the front door of the club. MacLeod shot the hippie dude a dirty look. *You and your fuckin' bone.*

"She comes in and says to me, 'Motherfucker, I don't ever wanna see you again.' And walks out. And I never saw her again."

Curious to learn how an old, striped chicken bone had rescued his manhood, MacLeod once more called upon the street smarts of Mr. Ernest Banks. He made his way out into the woods near Toano, past the magnolia tree, and told Banks what had happened.

"He says to me, 'You were in the presence of a black cat bone.' I'd been singing about that stuff a little bit, because the hippie chicks liked it. But I didn't really know what the hell it was. Then he told me how they made a black cat bone. Honeyboy Edwards verified this. When they make a black cat bone, they take a black cat and boil it. I don't know if it's alive or dead, but they boil it. When it's all boiled out, they strain it. They strain all that stuff through a colander or something, leaving the bones. They rinse the bones. Then, the person that knows the magic sucks on the bones until they find the sour one. That's the magic bone."

Logic dictates that anyone who has written several hundred songs has to have lived a little. In Doug's case, his fast times in Norfolk provided the stuff for more than a dozen.

He turned his introduction to the world of

hoodoo into "Bad Magic" and "Strip-Ed Bone." His knife-wielding prostitute friend became "Raylene." The one he loved was immortalized as "Nightbird."

"Rosa Lee," "East Carolina Woman," "My Black Pony" and "One Good Woman" suggest that the handsome young sailor hanging around the coffeehouses was getting his fair share.

But "A Broken Dream In A Broken Room" shows it wasn't all fun and games. This most confessional of MacLeod songs didn't appear on record until 2006.

"I doubt very much that most of the guys who are singing about these things have had experiences like that," the songwriter reflects. "And if younger musicians are singing about things they don't know about, well, they really shouldn't be doing that. They should be singing about what they know about. That's what the blues has always been."

* * *

GOD'S MUSIC

"Let me tell you one about Robert Junior Lockwood," says the storyteller, as talk turns to the spirituality of the blues.

Doug MacLeod remembers guitarist Lockwood – an important contributor to the blues canon during the mid-20th century, heard, for example, on Little Walter's "My Babe" and Sonny Boy Williamson's "Nine Below Zero" – as a cantankerous fellow. He claims Lockwood was generally wary of white musicians playing the blues and was cold to him initially. But when the two of them shared a venue and Lockwood liked what he heard from Doug, he softened a little.

"We were in the back room and I saw his twelve-string. I kept eyeing it, because I wanted to see where he tuned it to. Did he tune it down to a B or C or D? Which strings did he octavize and which strings did he not. And the gauge of the strings. Robert sees me looking at his guitar.

'You wanna play it?'

'I'd love to.'

'Lemme ask you something. What do you think about Robert Johnson, the Hellhound, the crossroads and all that?'

'To tell you the truth, Mr. Lockwood, I don't think too much of it. I think Robert Johnson had to be a helluva guitar player and he worked hard at it.'

Robert smiled and said: 'Go ahead and play.'"

The blues, for better or worse, is widely known as The Devil's Music – thanks in part to the apocryphal tale about guitar master Robert Johnson trading his soul for the extraordinary abilities he possessed. Doug MacLeod likes to think otherwise.

He has encountered the hoodoo and bad magic traditionally associated with the blues, and been witness to its inexplicable power. But on the whole, his personal experiences have tipped the scales heavily in the direction of the divine. Nearly every mystery he has been a part of, directly or indirectly, occurred on a plane much nearer to heaven than to hell.

The veteran bluesmen he learned from and grew to love were, to a man, spiritually inclined. Pee Wee Crayton, shortly before passing away, reportedly woke to tell his wife Esther about a pair of angels, Percy and Joe, who would come to take him home. Percy Mayfield and Big Joe Turner. It's a comforting thought.

MacLeod also relates how pianist Lloyd Glenn – a fellow member of George "Harmonica" Smith's band in the early 1980s – once told him that Patti Joy would give birth to a boy child long before Doug and his wife were even considering parenthood. He was so certain he even provided MacLeod with detailed instructions about how to give the baby boy "back to God" once he had been born: Doug was to take him to the highest hill at nighttime, raise him up to the heavens and give thanks to God for the gift.

Shortly after the birth of Doug's son Jesse, the two men bumped into one another at the Long Beach Blues Festival. It was the last time MacLeod ever saw Glenn, who died in May of 1985. He wanted to share the news of his blessed event, but the pianist beat him to the punch.

"You did have that boy child, didn't you?"

"Yeah, we just had it."

"I know. What's the boy's name?"

"Jesse."

"Did you do what I told you to do?"

"Yes, sir."

"He's gonna be alright."

Lockwood, Crayton, Glenn – none of them gave any credence to the old Devil's Music myth.

The story MacLeod tells about George "Harmonica" Smith and his passage from this earth is far more elaborate, its details verging on the supernatural. He shares it willingly, yet knows many will question his veracity and write off the events he describes as mere coincidence.

"If I heard you tell me this story, I would doubt it," he admits.

MacLeod's attachment to the man who nicknamed him Dubb provides some important context. George "Harmonica" Smith entered his life at a key juncture and, in the few years they shared stages and dressing rooms, gave him the fatherly affection he had longed for since childhood. (Remarkably, George Smith and William "Bally" MacLeod, Doug's father, were born on the same date just a few years apart.)

"In many ways, George was my father, in the sense that he gave me something I never got from my own father," MacLeod says.

When his natural father became gravely ill around 1996 – Doug, tellingly, cannot recall the exact date – he made a last-ditch effort to salvage their icy relationship. He flew to Florida to visit his dad at the hospital. The end was near. Doug's mom Dutchie tried in vain to get father and son to patch up their differences.

"Bally," she whispered to her dying husband, "Tell Doug that you love him. He's here."

MacLeod's father kept his mouth shut. She tried again.

"Bally, his hand is near you. Would you take his hand?"

Bally was alert, and understood, but did nothing.

"It hurt," says the spurned son two decades later. "At first, it hurt. And then I realized something. If he would have done that, it wouldn't have been true. It would have been for my mother. In a funny way, I respected him for it after the hurt passed. Whatever he was, he was."

The contrast between Doug's farewell to his biological father and the final hours he spent with George "Harmonica" Smith is startling.

Arriving at the LAC-USC Medical Center where the great musician would spend his final days, MacLeod came upon a man who no longer had his natural color. The history books say Smith was a few months shy of sixty; his wife Christine claims he was just 56. In any case, congenital heart disease had ravaged Smith's body. Yet Doug could see that his presence cheered his paternal friend.

"Hi Dubb."

"Hi George."

The two men talked a little. Then Smith asked him for a favor.

"Would you feed me?"

"Sure. Why? Don't you have a nurse?"

"I don't like my nurse, Dubb. She's mean."

Moments later, in walked the nurse. In pinched, nasally tones, she informed them that only family members were permitted to visit.

"This is my son," said Smith calmly.

"This is your *son*?" The nurse glanced at Doug, thinking, but not saying: *But he's white!*

"That's right. His name is Dubb. I want Dubb to feed me."

The nurse caved, brought a tray of food and barked instructions to leave it in the corner.

"She was such a miserable person," recalls MacLeod. "We laughed a little about that. Then George told me he was tired, so he slept a little." MacLeod stayed by him, and when Smith woke up, he fed him some more.

"Dubb, I want you to know something. I'm gonna teach you one more thing." MacLeod prepared to receive a final piece of musical advice. Smith had something else in mind.

"Dubb, I will say goodbye to you."

"OK, George. But I'll see you in a day or two."

"Just listen to me. I will say goodbye to you."

When Smith fell asleep again, MacLeod left. Two days later, his ersatz father passed.

"I heard about it and woke up Patti Joy and told her George was gone. She asked me what I wanted to do. I told her I felt we should go to Hermosa Beach. George and I had always played on the Redondo Beach Pier, but something told me we should go to Hermosa. So we drove there the next morning. We walked out on the pier. I was really missing George. I loved him."

Patti Joy and Doug MacLeod were looking northward on the pier when they noticed a seagull flying overhead. It circled a few times.

"Then he came down. Patti was standing next to me. The seagull sailed right past us and his wing touched my cheek."

The unexpected visitor then glided out over Santa Monica Bay, circled and moved on, leaving Doug speechless.

Patti Joy was the first to speak.

"Do you think?"

"No. That's a hell of a coincidence, Patti. There's no way that's . . . no."

"He did say he was gonna say goodbye to you."

Doug was reluctant to accept that George

"Harmonica" Smith had just flown by on sacred wing to bid him farewell – but a part of him wanted to believe it.

It wasn't until a few years later, after Jesse MacLeod was born, that the coincidences began to pile up.

"When Jesse was around five years old, Patti and Jesse were walking on Hermosa Beach. A seagull flies over. Jesse tugs at Patti's coat and says, 'Mommy, that looks like George.'"

Smith had passed away in October of 1983. Jesse was born the following year. At most, the boy had seen photos of George, who bore no resemblance to an aquatic bird.

"Nobody's going to believe it, but that's a true story," says MacLeod.

In the years since, he has repeatedly been visited by a lone seagull appearing out of the blue.

In his travels as a solo musician, he will often stop to photograph a picturesque stretch of coastline or a pleasing sunset. No seagulls in sight. Later, when he examines the results on his camera or phone, he'll find a single seagull has photo-bombed the shot. This has happened in Brittany and on the Mersey River in Liverpool and along the Pacific Coast Highway on the way to Ventura. MacLeod has the evidence to prove it.

"Another time I was driving up to Ventura to do a gig and I stopped off at Ralphs Supermarket to get a little something to hold me over. I do that, get back in the car, pull out of the parking spot, about to drive off, but there's a seagull standing right in the way. Just standing there. I honk the horn. It doesn't move. The people behind me start honking their horns. There are like three cars behind me wondering why I'm not moving. So finally, I roll down the window and holler: 'George, will you get out of the way?' And the seagull flew!"

Is the bird he has encountered in France, England, California and elsewhere MacLeod's guardian angel? Did God send George to watch over him? Do Doug's experiences suggest that bluesmen, for all their flaws and failings, might just be on the fast track to heaven?

"I don't know how to explain it. I just know that George has always been with me. He never, ever let me go. It's been that way ever since he said, 'There's one more thing I've got to teach you.' It's a side of this music you don't hear much about."

* * *

GOING HOME

"Once, when I had my band back in the 80s, I was approached by a guy named Jim Halsey. He's a big-time agent who handles The Oak Ridge Boys, Roy Clark, people like that. He was interested in managing me, so we set up a meeting at some fancy hotel in Santa Monica."

The exchange Doug MacLeod is referring to took place some 25 years ago, so the details are a little fuzzy. But he remembers, clear as day, the thrust of his conversation with the noted impresario, who has served on the boards of the Country Music Association and National Academy of Recording Arts and Sciences.

"He said, 'Would you like to be a star?' I thought about it for a second and told him I wasn't sure. A part of me inside wanted to say yes, so I could throw it back at my father. But a bigger part said maybe not. I remembered what my other father George had told me to do and that was to play my original blues for the people."

As the talk between the two men progressed, Halsey informed MacLeod that he would probably have to make some changes to his music to ensure success.

"I told him I didn't think I could do that. All I really wanted to do was to touch people and make them feel better. He looked at me and said, 'I'd like to help you, but I don't think I can.' He said it in a very sensitive way, but still, my heart sank."

Halsey had come in expecting to find a man with dollar signs in his eyes. But he quickly understood where MacLeod was coming from and where he wanted to go. Ultimately, he would put a positive spin on the musician's decision to forego stardom and follow his true calling.

"He told me something I have never forgotten," says Doug. "Jim said, 'Not everybody is going to know you. But that's OK. That means you can go to the grocery store, a ballgame or a movie without being pounced on. The people that do recognize you will shake your hand and thank you for what you do. And that's not a bad thing at all, is it?' I said, no, it's not. Turns out, he was right."

MacLeod stuck to his guns that day in Santa Monica. Today, he is reaping the benefits. At the supermarket, at the ballpark, at the merchandise table – the expressions of thanks he receives from fans close to home and around the world feel like money in his pocket.

"I think about Jim every time it happens and now it's happening more."

Fast forward nearly three decades: MacLeod is recounting the tale of his business lunch with Jim Halsey at a loud and decidedly less swanky hotel restaurant in Hamburg, Germany. There's a spicy Cajun chicken dish on the table in front of him, a pile of smudged napkins, a bottle of Tabasco and a tall, cold beer at arm's length. The server is a young, caramel-skinned beauty with million-dollar dimples.

"You've got a great personality," beams MacLeod during one of her visits. It is not a come-on. He is comfortable in his skin, comfortable with his age. A man wholly dedicated to brightening up peoples' days.

"I hope you never change."

The waitress, in imperfect English, responds to him with a sentiment no writer could have scripted any better.

"The world is so hard sometimes. But it's good to smile."

Yes. It is good to smile. And MacLeod, seven-plus decades into his journey on this earth, has found plenty to smile about.

"It seems to me that I've lived two lives," he reflects. "My earlier life – which stopped when I met George – and the life I've lived ever since meeting George until right now. I feel so fortunate that God has given me some years until the end of my life where I am still strong. Still healthy. I have more power and more energy than I did when I was in my thirties."

The first act of Doug's story – roughly half a life, give or take a few years – was troubled to say the least. The traumas of childhood left him messed up in so many ways, he says, he didn't know whether he was coming or going.

The second act, on the other hand, has been imbued with purpose, rich with experiences, full of friendships and anchored by a satisfying and harmonious family environment. How did he get there? He's not completely sure.

"Sometimes I look at my life and go: Wow, what the hell has been going on? Maybe I did get more out of that weed than Chinese food!"

At 72, he is content to stay at home much of the time, following the ins and outs of the long baseball season and the exploits of his beloved St. Louis Cardinals. He and his wife Patti Joy have called the South Bay section of Los Angeles home for well over 30 years now, but like any true fan, he has never switched allegiances. Son Jesse lives in nearby Hollywood and is making a name for himself as a soulful singer-songwriter.

"Blues is not his main thing, but all his music has blues in it," observes the elder MacLeod. "I'm just so proud of him."

When Jesse was in his early twenties, before his musical pursuits really began to take root, he gave his dad the greatest gift any child can give a parent.

"I was playing a local club with some friends of mine," Doug MacLeod recalls. "Denny Croy on bass. Dave Kida on drums. Jesse came in and said he had something to tell me. This was between songs. So I'm thinking something bad had happened, like he'd been in an accident with the car. I asked him if everything was alright. He said, 'I just came by to tell you you've been a wonderful dad.'"

Jesse's expression of gratitude felt like a moment of arrival. Doug could now look back on his checkered family history and know that in his own parenting efforts, at least, and against all odds, he had gotten things right.

"Every once in a while you fall into a bowl of whipped cream," he says, taking none of the credit.

Those local gigs he used to do in and around Los Angeles have become a thing of the past. Occasionally he'll do a one-off duo or trio show for the DubbHeads and for the sheer enjoyment of playing. He still does plenty of touring, though, appearing at clubs, theaters and festivals throughout the United States and crossing the Atlantic a couple of times each year to reach his many fans in Europe. He is on his own the majority of the time, and it can be a grind no matter how nice the scenery is or how many old cathedrals he visits.

"I think blues guys are a different ilk," he says about the workmanlike attitude he shares with most of his contemporaries. "Once, James Harman was talking to an interviewer about what it's like to be a blues musician. He said we're like truck drivers. We drive. We unload. But that's where it stops, because then we play and load up again and drive off again."

MacLeod admits he doesn't like to get behind the wheel at night anymore. While on the road, he's careful about his vitamin intake, doesn't overdo it with the beer and tries to avoid red meat. In fact, it's written into his tour rider.

"I have two doctors," he explains. "A general practitioner and one who checks out my colon. They are both fans of my music and say they'll do their best to keep me on the planet as long as they can. So I follow their advice."

In that regard, he has set himself a lofty goal: He would like to outlast his friend David "Honeyboy"

Edwards. Edwards lived to be 96 and could find his way around a fretboard until the very end. He was booked to play a gig in Chicago on the day he died.

Obviously, MacLeod thinks about his own mortality, even as he approaches his mid-seventies in good mental and physical shape.

"Sure I think about it. Like when you realize there's more behind you than what's in front of you. Those sayings like youth is wasted on the young – now you start to understand what that means."

The unaccompanied vocal performance "Going Home" from his award-winning *Break The Chain* album expresses his coming to terms with the realities of life and death.

"This is gonna sound simple," he says, "but I look at it one day at a time. If my time comes tomorrow – as it says in the song – there ain't nothin' I can do about. I can't go to the conductor and say, look, can I get an extension on this ticket? Once you realize that, you try to live each day as if it's your whole life, and fill it up. So that if you have to go, you go with no regrets."

MacLeod can thankfully say that his list of grievances is small.

When his father Bally passed away and mother Dutchie followed him some years later, there was no Hollywood ending awaiting him. Things were left unsaid. Broken relationships remained unreconciled. MacLeod's father in particular never accepted his involvement in what he called Negro music. He even left physical evidence behind.

"After my mother died," recalls MacLeod, "my wife and I went back to clear out the house. We found all of my CDs and albums. They were all shrink-wrapped. They never listened to one of them. Not one. That hurt."

There's a similar story about celebrated jazz cornetist Bix Beiderbecke, who made roughly 160 recordings between 1924 and 1930. Beiderbecke's strict Teutonic parents never got used to their son devoting his talents and energy to what they considered to be "low-class" music. Before succumbing to alcoholism in New York at age 28, Beiderbecke was visiting the family home in Davenport, Iowa, and stumbled upon all the records he had sent home, unopened, in a dusty closet.

"Patti and I were watching the Ken Burns *Jazz* miniseries when I found that out about Bix Beiderbecke. That his parents had never listened to his records. I turned to Patti and said, 'Well, I'm in damn good company.'"

Meanwhile, MacLeod's regard for the music that essentially became his home and safe haven remains undeterred. He realizes certain people will always consider the blues to be a simple or even primitive form of art. He knows differently and gladly answers the naysayers with some variation of an often-used saying: The blues may be simple, but it sure ain't easy.

"This music is not something you look at and go, 'Three chords? I can do that!' There's a lot more going on than that."

For him, the blues, at its core, remains a music of overcoming adversity, not subjecting to adversity.

"I really believe that. When you really stop to think about who created it and the conditions under which it was created, that speaks volumes. I hope we never lose sight of that. That's where it comes from."

* * *

Is Doug MacLeod a household name? Hardly. Those who move on the fringes of mainstream culture, far removed from the pop charts – as blues musicians clearly do – are unfamiliar to the vast majority of consumers. Even the talented and passionate artists currently defining the blues genre, where MacLeod has indeed achieved considerable fame, reach only a small percentage of the fans and marketplace.

Yet his success can be measured in other terms. For one, he is doing exactly what he told Jim Halsey he wanted to do. It's the one thing he feels he was put on this earth for: to play his music for the people and to make them feel better than they did before. Whether it's an audience of 20, 200 or 2000, each time MacLeod takes the stage, he opens new eyes to the undeniable beauty and expressive power of the blues.

And if he ever wants to prove beyond the shadow of a doubt that the blues is truly a music of overcoming adversity, then he can offer his own, bumpy, ultimately satisfying journey as exhibit A.

"I really have no regrets. I have a wonderful wife. A wonderful son. There is love in my life. For the first time in my life, there is love. Real, honest-to-goodness love."

Still traveling on the unmarked road, Doug MacLeod now looks around and likes what he sees.

"If someone had told me when I was 21, look, here's what's gonna happen: You're gonna have all this tribulation at the beginning of your life, but the last part of your life is gonna be like it is now. You still wanna do it? I'd say: In a heartbeat."

* * *

Dubb, 2014.

(Photo: Theo Looijmans)

FROM THE ARCHIVES: BERLIN 2002

(*Author's note*: It's true. There really is only one first time. When I sat down to interview Doug MacLeod in 2002, around the time of his *A Little Sin* album, he was in the mood to "let stuff out," as he says. As we shared a pint of Köstritzer Black Lager, he revealed some of the intricacies of his guitar tunings, spoke about the songs from his current record and told funny stories about working as a radio DJ. But what fascinated me most of all were his tales of coming of age in late seventies Los Angeles, where he became the "white nigga mothafucka" who played with the darker-complexioned big boys who ruled the roost. As I sat there, soaking it all in, I knew I'd be unable to use much of it in my article – assigned to me by a German blues quarterly – and that, even if I could, his colloquial speech as well as that of his Los Angeles blues compadres would get lost in translation. Here, for the first time anywhere, is the entire interview, conducted on November 6th 2002 at the Yorckschlösschen in Berlin, Germany. – VA)

Vincent Abbate: I've been trying to get a feel for the progression your music has taken in the past 20 years. In the 1980s, you put out band albums that were mostly electric with a funky, jazzy feel. Then in 1994, you had *Come To Find.* That and everything since has been primarily acoustic, country blues. Where did that change come from?

Doug MacLeod: I started out as an acoustic player, then went to the electric blues, and I like jazz, too. I'm a big Kenny Burrell fan. I wanted to do that, did it with my band and liked it. But something happened. I felt myself being pulled back to my roots. Pulled back to that old man I met in Virginia. One of the times where it happened, I'll never forget it. I was with George "Harmonica" Smith; we were out on the road somewhere in Northern California. He said: "Dubb, let's play some blues together." He took me in the hotel room. We were sharing a room. He started singing "Key to the Highway." He told me Big Bill Broonzy was his favorite singer. I said, "Gee, I used to love Big Bill Broonzy." He said, "Oh, really?" He thought I was just an electric player.
George and I played, and it hit really good. I really liked it. It kind of lay dormant for a while and then it surfaced. I remember telling my wife, "I think I wanna go acoustic." She said, "Well, go." But there

are no acoustic guys in Los Angeles. It's a very small market. She said if that's what in your heart, do it. So that's how it happened. I just stopped one day. One of my songs is about this. It's called "Unmarked Road." I wrote that song about doing something and all of a sudden, you realize you don't wanna spend the rest of your life doing that. Even though you're going to take chances or you might miss things, it's a scary thing. But you know you gotta get on that unmarked road. Get on it and go. So far – knock on wood – it's turned out to be a really good decision. But it was a heartfelt thing.

VA: *Come To Find* was also your first record with Joe Harley as producer. Was that a coincidence, or did he have something to do with the change of direction?

DM: I was one of the pall bearers when Big Joe Turner died. I was one of his favorite guitar players. His wife told me that and I was honored. So I'm standing at the grave and this guy from the Big Joe Turner foundation asked me if I'd ever heard of AudioQuest. I said no. "Well," he said, "They like what you do. Why don't you send Joe Harley a tape? Joe called me back. That's how that happened. I've since left AudioQuest. Joe is no longer with the label. There were some changes made. AudioQuest is with Valley

Entertainment now. They're fine, but we didn't quite see eye to eye, and it was time to move.

VA: Can you tell me about your bandmates Denny Croy and Dave Kida?

DM: I'd be glad to. First of all, no one is going to believe this, but we never rehearse. We rehearsed one time for *Whose Truth, Whose Lies* because Rich DelGrosso was playing mandolin. So Rich came to Dave's house and we took about two and a half hours to rehearse. Every other time we've played, I don't even tell Denny what key it is. He just picks it up. With Dave, I just start up and he picks up the feel. And we invent songs. I don't write out any chord changes or anything. But they follow me. They are the most intuitive musicians I've ever worked with. I would love to bring them over to Europe if the economics allow.

VA: So most of your gigs in the States are as a trio?

DM: No, mostly solo or duo with Denny on bass.

VA: What about "East Texas Sugar" on the new record *A Little Sin*? Is that Denny with you or is it all you?

DM: That's all me.

VA: How did you do that?!

DM: That's a God-given gift. You know, my right hand is different than most guys' right hands. I've got a weird right hand. It's a good one. But that just came to me. Denny and I were working and we got done with it and we were playing some club and I looked at him and said, "You know Denny, I don't really need you on that." He says: "You know what? You don't." So when we play together, all Denny does is hit a big ol' G. I put it in a weird tuning, which almost sounds like Ravi Shankar meets the Delta. That's a tuning that came to me; I just invented that. It was the tuning that the song needed.

VA: You just said the magic word. Tuning!

DM: I call the tuning on "East Texas Sugar" Too Many Gs. I've got Bastard G, Too Many Gs, Too Many Ds, Open D, Drop D, Open G.

VA: How do you find the right tuning for a song?

DM: That's a gift. That doesn't come from me. I think

that comes from a higher power. I've always felt that the songs that come to me, when they come, I think they're gifts. And if I don't get it, it'll go down to the next guy. Do you understand what I'm saying? They come.
The funny thing is, of all the songs I've written – I can remember them all. The melodies, everything. And I've written about 325 songs. I might mess up the words, but the melodies, the feel . . . it's like there's a computer in me.

VA: Are you going to do "East Texas Sugar" tonight?

DM: I'll see if I can get to that Too Many Gs tuning. If I get there. And if I can get back out!

VA: "Devilment Doin' Woman" reminds me of a Skip James song.

DM: Perfect. You heard it exactly right. It's a Skip James feel. It's not in his open D-minor tuning. That's a Bastard G tuning. But I got it capoed up on the fourth fret.

VA: I'm glad I play some guitar, because if you were a harmonica player and you just said that to me in harmonica terms, I would have no idea what you're talking about! Unfair question, but how many takes did you need for "New Panama Limited"?

DM: One. That's Joe Harley's way. Joe comes from the old school. Remember the old Fantasy, Prestige and Blue Note records? Where they just put the mic up and the guys played it? That's where Joe comes from. So you gotta know the songs when you go into a Joe Harley session. "Panama" was one take. Some of the others might have been two takes. But Joe only says stuff like, "OK. We got that one. Let's see if there's a better one."

VA: What is the source for "Panama Limited," which you credit to Bukka White?

DM: But it really isn't. The Bukka White version doesn't sound anything like it. The first version I heard was from Tom Rush, a folk singer from Boston. As I've traveled, I've heard that Tom actually opened for Bukka White after he'd been rediscovered. Apparently, Bukka White wrote about eight or nine songs about trains. The story I heard is that Tom Rush incorporated them all into one that he called the "Panama Limited." Of all the train songs, I think that's the most romantic title, because it's not even in Panama and it's running from New Orleans to

Chicago. I think in Tom Rush's version it's running from somewhere else.
I heard that and thought, well, that's like a folk song. I started doing pretty much the Tom Rush version. Then I met people like Honeyboy Edwards, who I mention in the song, and we talked about him and Joe Williams, Robert Johnson riding those trains and the guy I met, somewhere they told me he worked on the City of New Orleans train. I said, let me put this all into a song and call it the "New Panama Limited" and keep the tradition of the old one. So the actual lineage is Bukka White to Tom Rush to me.
And if some guy – maybe even tonight – hears it and goes "God, I like that song," maybe there will be another continuation. You understand what I'm saying?

VA: One more question about a song off the album – the shortest one.

DM: "The Last Blues Song Ever Wrote"? We were in the studio, and sometimes, especially when you do a record in two days, there's a lot of pressure. The engineers are always looking to see if maybe you've got one they're not expecting. I was having a little fun. I said, "Joe, I've got one."
So they get the tape rolling. I do the introduction,

sing “I didn’t wake up this morning,” and that was it. They go, “Doug, was that it?” I said yeah. “What’s the name of that?” “The Last Blues Song Ever Wrote.” I said to Joe, with my luck, that’ll be the song that gets all the airplay and I’ll make 28 cents every time it’s played.

VA: Do you still do your radio show?

DM: Yup. I tape them. It’s all real time. So I just put the DAT tape in and I run it for five hours. If there’s mistakes, I leave them. Somebody asked me why I do that. These people listening to me know me. If they hear a five-hour show with Doug MacLeod and it’s perfect, they’ll know it’s on tape. You got to make a little mistake somewhere! You hit the wrong button or the wrong song comes up, that’s all a part of live radio. And I think people enjoy that.
Here’s a cute story. I’m answering the phone. I pick up and say KKJZ, can I help you? The lady asks if it’s Doug MacLeod and asks me what I’m doing. I said I’m playing music. She says yeah, but this is a slow song. I said yeah. She says, well I’m having a hard time keeping my husband up. I said madam, I don’t think that’s my problem!

VA: What do you play on the show?

DM: I like to think of it as "river music." If it came off the river or is a child of the Mississippi, that's music I tend towards. But I play Tyrone Davis. I play soul. I come from the St. Louis area, and I heard that stuff. I like Little Milton. You're gonna hear Sleepy John Estes. Ray Charles.

VA: So Doug MacLeod has a format.

DM: This is my criteria. I don't like guys that sing verses like "My baby left me, I'm so blue, my baby left me, I don't know what to do," then play eight choruses of diarrhea guitar. Do you understand what I mean? I don't play it. To me, that's not blues. It never was.

My honest opinion? The old guys I played with and learned it from – if you played like that – they could hurt you. You understand what I mean? That's the thing that bothers me. There's not enough guys left to say "motherfucker". What I mean by that is: When I was coming up in the blues, you didn't play too many notes. If I was jiving, they would take me in the back and say, "Motherfucker, don't you play like that again or I'll break your motherfuckin' face."

Now, somebody talks to you like that, you gonna sit up and take notice, right? Especially when you're skinnier than them and afraid of them. So I don't play that.

And I think a guy gotta sing. He's gotta sing. I don't care what color you are, because I don't believe in that color stuff.

That's not because I'm a white guy. I believe it's human music. I believe that everybody has the blues. Everybody. I don't care if you're from Europe, the United States, Mississippi, I don't care. Because we all have the same feelings. Everybody wants to be loved. Everybody wants to have savings for your family. Everybody wants good things for themselves. You know what I mean?

I have a saying. If people ask, well, how do you get the blues? I say: Just get born and the blues will find you. Because it's part of life. One of the greatest times I ever had in my life was not in a nightclub. It was sitting in Brownie McGhee's garage, drinking Coca-Cola, playing music together. Talking and watching him and learning from him. Hearing him talk about the blues is truth. And thinking about years ago when I met Willie Dixon. This is a great story.

I was sitting at this tribute to Shakey Jake Harris at the Palamino Club in North Hollywood. Willie Dixon sat down right next to me. I was really taken aback by it. If you're a songwriter, it's like being a baseball player and Henry Aaron sits down next to you. So I was quiet. Shy. He leaned over to me and said, "Are you Doug MacLeod?" I said yeah. He said, "You wrote 'Grease In My Gravy,' didn't you?" I said yeah! We shook hands and got to talking. And he liked my songwriting. You can't get a higher compliment than that.

So I asked him: "Mr. Dixon, what is the blues for you?" I told him how much I loved his music, that there was always humor and sadness in it. He said blues is the true facts of life. That was it. There was no color there. He didn't say the blues is the true facts of black life. He said blues is the true facts of life.

So if you look at it that way, it's everybody. We all have those true facts of life. That's some powerful stuff. All that goes into what I think about when I'm playing. Those are the criteria. There are some good guys out there.

VA: Do you want to mention some names?

DM: Chris Cain is one of my favorites. I don't think he gets enough recognition. He writes, sings and plays. The old guys used to say that. When I was sitting down with Ernest Banks, I asked him one time, I said I wanted to be a bluesman. This is after he and I became friends. At first, he didn't want any part of me. He didn't trust me. But after he started to see I was really after that music and that philosophy he was teaching.

I remember we sat down one time at the Folk Ghetto in Norfolk, Virginia, on Freemason Street. We're sitting on the corner, as we did many times. I would always bring a bottle of Chianti wine. I asked him: "Mr. Banks, tell me something. You said that if I'm gonna be a bluesman, I gotta play, write and sing. I've never been to Mississippi and I don't know much about mojos and black cat bones and mystery mud and goober dust. The stuff that I've learned, I've learned from you, and it scares me to death. And I don't even know if I wanna know any more about it. So what am I gonna do?"

He looked at me with that one eye he had and said: "Have you ever been lonely?" I said yes. "You ever need rent money for that little place you got?" I said yes. "You ever need a woman's touch?" I said yes. He said that's the blues, too, boy. You can write about that. A great lesson, isn't it?

When you get it from someone like that, one of the old guys that really did it, that's like going to a masters class in college. Sitting down with one of the masters that's teaching you not the notes, but the philosophy. He didn't ever give me the notes. He looked at me, and if I got it, I was supposed to. And if I didn't, fuck 'im. Once he got to know me, it was a little better. He might go, "Well, you might wanna do that over there."

VA: I'm thinking about what you said before. About that "motherfucker" thing.

DM: That's how they were. Those guys were rough. And if you played wrong . . . you're the only white face in a black club and they're calling you motherfucker? That's gonna scare you to deff – with two effs. You *will* play less. You will play less and make each note count.

VA: How did they show their approval? That they'd accepted you.

DM: They called me nigger. The highest compliment I ever got.

VA: I wonder if I can print that.

DM: Print it! It's time for people to know. Once, Pee Wee Crayton put his arm around me after a show and said, "You are one white nigga muthafucka." That was the highest compliment – for him to say, "You play like a nigger, boy." Then, later on, when I had enough courage, and they told me I was alright for a white boy, I would say: "I ain't a boy. I'm a man. And I'm good for any man."

* * *

ABOUT THE AUTHOR

New York-born author and journalist Vincent Abbate has been an important voice on the international blues and roots music scene for over 20 years. His interviews, columns and reviews have appeared in leading print magazines including *Blues Revue* and *Blues Music Magazine* (US), *The Blues* (UK), *bluesnews* and *ROCKS* (DE). His popular blog *Who Is Blues* launched in 2017.

If you've enjoyed your time in the pages of *Who Is Blues Vol. 1*, please take a moment to leave a review where you purchased it online and help spread the word on social media – or even in the real world.

To stay informed of future volumes in the *Who Is Blues* series, please sign up for the Who Is Blues email newsletter at **www.whoisblues.com**.

ACKNOWLEDGEMENTS

My sincere thanks go to the following individuals, whose efforts were vital to the completion of this book: Miki Mulvehill, Theo & Diana Looijmans, Patti Joy MacLeod, Jesse MacLeod, Karen Proeme, Volker Bredow, Stephan "Mc" Ebel and Jorma & Vanessa Kaukonen.

Special thanks to Joe Abbate for starting the ball rolling two summers ago.

A word of appreciation to authors Peter Guralnick and Roger Angell, whose way with words first inspired me to try my hand at non-fiction.

Finally, my deepest gratitude goes to Doug MacLeod for his trust, openness, patience, humor and friendship. And most of all, for his gift of music.

Made in United States
North Haven, CT
26 October 2022